BOB DYLAN THE LYRICS 1961

# ROUGH AND
# ROWDY WAYS
# 粗野风格

## 鲍勃·迪伦诗歌集 1961—2020
### VOL.10

[美] 鲍勃·迪伦 著  李皖 顾悦 译

中信出版集团 | 北京

## 共度此生
## TOGETHER THROUGH LIFE

## 粗野风格
## ROUGH AND ROWDY WAYS

# TOGETHER THROUGH LIFE
## 共度此生

Life is for Love — all try say that comes Blind
If you want to live Easy baby — mine —

What the use of all my dreaming, I must have better things to do
Various dreams wunda for me my they

You just as whour was Ever — baby you cant stint
I must losing my mind

(Pleading) James Joyce (Fan
People —

Everybody got all the money / Everybody beautiful clothes
Everybody got flowers i dont even a simple rose

《共度此生》是迪伦第33张录音室专辑，由哥伦比亚唱片公司发行于2009年4月28日，出版一周即"空降"为多个国家的排行榜冠军，包括美国和英国。

除1首歌词外，其他9首均系迪伦与罗伯特·亨特合写，后者是感恩而死乐队（Grateful Dead）的词作者。

《人世维艰》是迪伦应法国导演奥利维耶·达昂（Olivier Dahan）之邀，为其电影《我自己的情歌》（*My Own Love Song*，2010）写的插曲，它构成了迪伦这张专辑的动机。电影讲述下肢瘫痪、早已匿迹歌坛的女歌手简的故事。有一天，她接到儿子来信，邀请她参加第一次圣餐会。在好友乔伊的鼓励下，简踏上了前往新奥尔良的长旅，并在旅途中创作出了最动人的歌曲。

当到达圣餐处时，简担心在她因事故昏迷7年后儿子已认不出她。乔伊让她唱歌。于是简唱起这首《人世维艰》，正准备离开的儿子站在了她的面前。

摇滚乐评人丹·恩格勒（Dan Engler）撰文指出："鲍勃·迪伦声称，在1997年录制他里程碑式的专辑《被遗忘的时光》时，他感觉到巴迪·霍利（Buddy Holly）一直在录制现场。在他的新专辑《共度此生》中，你能感到迪伦的老朋友道格·萨姆（Doug Sahm，1941—1999）的魂灵飘荡在录音的整个过程中。"[1]

道格·萨姆是一位得州音乐家，20世纪60年代即活跃在美国乐坛，从迷幻民谣到乡村布鲁斯，从城市布鲁斯到得式 – 墨式摇滚乐——他一生的道路，确实有点像迪伦在此专辑中穿越过的一个个音乐风格。

这张专辑像是回到了20世纪40年代，乐手们开着老式车穿过美国南部，一直驶向墨西哥的边疆小镇。来自墨式布鲁斯摇滚劲旅——狼乐队（Los Lobos）的戴维·伊达尔戈（David Hidalgo）用一台手风琴，来自汤姆·佩蒂和心碎者乐队的迈克·坎贝尔（Mike Campbell）用一把电吉他，制作出了迪伦需要的"路易斯安那 – 墨西哥"之音，一种老美国"国境之南"的风情。

10首歌曲均以年迈苍老的声音演唱，歌词也有一种年迈苍老的调子，录音听起来像是至少半个世纪以前的。作为歌手，迪伦一出生即苍老，仿佛阅尽人事的民间智慧老人，但这张专辑的苍老，尤其像是覆盖了这位歌手一生的重重岁月：既绝望，又火热；既白发苍苍，又燃起了末路、末世的熊熊涅槃之火，采用当时已经基本上弃用的歌曲体裁、演奏方式和录音效果。但这黑暗、末路的声音里却又含有一丝安慰。其中的情歌，依然是火热的。

从歌词看，这些歌曲非常枯涩，话很少。这甚至让人怀疑，若是没有另一位老人（罗伯特·亨特），迪伦压根没有说话的冲动，更不会有灵感出现。这些歌词从一首首历

---

[1] "Dylan delivers South of the Border flavor on Together Through Life". *Verde Independent*. Retrieved May 28, 2021.

史老歌那里获得了动机，异常干瘪，全是收缩性的，没有丝毫飞扬之意。若是没有外界的强力刺激，没有两位老人的互动，这些歌词会不会缩成一个个原点？但是，歌词中的这些话，非常缓慢，非常不顺畅，又非常有分量，像冬日冷风中苦楝树上未落下的最后的果实。

时隔 3 年，《共度此生》带着挣扎之意，与迪伦的上一张专辑《摩登时代》几乎没有共同之处。我曾经评价迪伦的后期作品是"道成肉身"。一个时代人物，把自己活成了他最大的作品。因为迪伦丰富的人生阅历，他历经的一个个非凡年代，都构成了他晚年写作的幽深背景——哪怕是一首短歌，由此也具有了非同一般的长度、厚度、复杂性和重量，像其整个人生一样意味深长。

迪伦重回美国民歌史上的老歌样式，眼睛却注视着前方。这些歌基本上不是回忆，而是诉说着既像现在正包围着他，又像缠绕着他一生的感受，都不是什么好感受——周遭世界充满了欺骗、丑恶和危险，隐隐有说不出的噩兆，似乎越变越坏。从中你能听到这老人的悲哀和失望，他好像历经了劫难，已经精疲力竭。然而这歌声终究又让人坚定，就像科里·杜布罗瓦（Corey duBrowa）说的："当一生的抱负和成就被变幻之风卷走时，爱——以及我们在共同痛苦中找到的安慰——本质上就是我们剩下的一切。"[1]

该专辑于加州好莱坞的录音室录制，时间为 2008 年10 月，录音场次不详。

---

[1]  duBrowa, Corey (April 28, 2009). "Bob Dylan: Together Through Life". *Paste*. Archived from the original on April 29, 2009. Retrieved January 28, 2018.

## BEYOND HERE LIES NOTHIN'
(WITH ROBERT HUNTER)

I love you pretty baby
You're the only love I've ever known
Just as long as you stay with me
The whole world is my throne
Beyond here lies nothin'
Nothin' we can call our own

I'm movin' after midnight
Down boulevards of broken cars
Don't know what I'd do without it
Without this love that we call ours
Beyond here lies nothin'
Nothin' but the moon and stars

Down every street there's a window
And every window made of glass
We'll keep on lovin' pretty baby
For as long as love will last
Beyond here lies nothin'

## 在此之外一无所有 [1]

（与罗伯特·亨特合作）

我爱你小美人儿
你是我知道的，唯一的爱
只要你在身边陪着
全世界就是我的王座
在此之外一无所有
再无一物堪称我们所有

午夜已过
我在尽是破车的林荫道走着
不知道没有了我们宣称的爱
我还能干什么
在此之外一无所有
除了星星和这一轮明月

每条大街都有一扇窗
每扇窗都是玻璃做的
我们将爱下去小美人儿
一直爱到爱能持续的最后
在此之外一无所有

---

[1] 本张专辑均由郝佳校译。

But the mountains of the past

My ship is in the harbor
And the sails are spread
Listen to me pretty baby
Lay your hand upon my head
Beyond here lies nothin'
Nothin' done and nothin' said

除了那往昔的连绵山岳

我的船正在海港
帆已升起就要启航
听我说小美人儿
请把手放在我头上
在此之外一无所有
什么都没做，什么也都未讲

## LIFE IS HARD
### (WITH ROBERT HUNTER)

The evening winds are still
I've lost the way and will
Can't tell you where they went
I just know what they meant
I'm always on my guard
Admitting life is hard
Without you near me

The friend you used to be
So near and dear to me
You slipped so far away
Where did we go astray
I pass the old schoolyard
Admitting life is hard
Without you near me

Ever since the day
The day you went away

## 人世维艰 [1]

（与罗伯特·亨特合作）

夜风沉寂

路途和意愿已失

我说不清它们去往何处

只体会到其中含义

一直以来小心翼翼

无奈接受这人世维艰

没有你在身边


你一度是我朋友

这么近，这么亲

不知不觉却悄然远离

是在哪儿我们步入了岔路

我走过昔日校园

无奈接受这人世维艰

没有你在身边


自从那一天

你走的那一天

---

[1] 这首是迪伦为美法联合制作的公路电影《我自己的情歌》(*My Own Love Song*, 2010) 而作的歌曲。

I felt that emptiness so wide

I don't know what's wrong or right

I just know I need strength to fight

Strength to fight that world outside


Since we've been out of touch

I haven't felt that much

From day to barren day

My heart stays locked away

I walk the boulevard

Admitting life is hard

Without you near me


The sun is sinking low

I guess it's time to go

I feel a chilly breeze

In place of memories

My dreams are locked and barred

Admitting life is hard

Without you near me

我感到空虚如此寥廓
我辨不清孰是孰非
只知道我需要力量回击
回击这外面的世界

自从失去联系
不再有多少感觉
萧索日甚一日
这内心已然封闭
我在林荫大道徘徊
无奈接受这人世维艰
没有你在身边

太阳西沉
是时候要走了
我觉出一股冷风
取代了记忆
梦已上锁，关上围栏
无奈接受这人世维艰
没有你在身边

## MY WIFE'S HOME TOWN
(WITH ROBERT HUNTER)


Well I didn't come here to deal with a doggone thing
I just came here to hear the drummer's cymbal ring
There ain't no way you can put me down
I just want to say that Hell's my wife's home town

Well there's reasons for that and reasons for this
I can't think of any just now, but I know they exist
I'm sitting in the sun 'til my skin turns brown
I just want to say that Hell's my wife's home town
Home town, home town

She can make you steal, make you rob
Give you the hives, make you lose your job
Make things bad, she can make things worse
She got stuff more potent than a gypsy curse

One of these days, I'll end up on the run

## 我老婆家乡

（与罗伯特·亨特合作）

好吧，我来这儿不是为了处理屁事儿
我来这儿是为了听那鼓手的铙钹响
你甭想叫我不开心
我只告诉你这可是他妈的我老婆家乡

好吧，这个有理，那个也有理
我现在想不起来，可我知道它们存在
我坐在阳光中，直到皮肤晒成小麦色
我只告诉你这可是他妈的我老婆家乡
家乡，家乡

她能够让你偷，还能够让你抢
给你荨麻疹，让你失业
能让事情变糟，让事情糟上加糟
她有的玩意儿可比吉卜赛咒语有效

终有一天，我会逃亡

I'm pretty sure, she'll make me kill someone
I'm going inside, roll the shutters down
I just want to say that Hell's my wife's home town

Well there's plenty to remember, plenty to forget
I still can remember the day we met
I lost my reason long ago
My love for her is all I know

State gone broke, the county's dry
Don't be looking at me with that evil eye
Keep on walking, don't be hanging around
I'm telling you again that Hell's my wife's home town
Home town, home town

我很确定，她会叫我杀人 [1]
我会走进去，摇下百叶窗
我只告诉你这可是他妈的我老婆家乡

好吧，太多事要记住，太多事要忘记
我还记得我们相遇的日子
很早以前我便失去了理智
我对她的爱是我知道的一切

州已破碎，县已干涸
别用那恶眼瞪我
往前走好了，别再磨叽
我再说一次，这可是他妈的我老婆家乡
家乡，家乡

---

[1] "终有一天，我会逃亡 / 我很确定，她会叫我杀人"，引自戴维·赖特（David Wright）译乔叟小说《坎特伯雷故事》（*The Canterbury Tales*）"僧士的故事"篇。

## IF YOU EVER GO TO HOUSTON
(WITH ROBERT HUNTER)


If you ever go to Houston

Better walk right

Keep your hands in your pockets

And your gun-belt tight

You'll be asking for trouble

If you're lookin' for a fight

If you ever go to Houston

Boy, you better walk right


If you're ever down there

On Bagby and Lamar

You better watch out for

The man with the shining star

Better know where you're going

Or stay where you are

If you're ever down there

## 如果有天你去休斯敦

（与罗伯特·亨特合作）


如果有天你去休斯敦

最好乖乖走路

手要插在口袋里

枪带要系紧

你会自讨苦吃

如果你想干仗

如果有天你去休斯敦

小子，你最好乖乖走路 [1]


如果有天你到了那儿

到了巴格比和拉马尔 [2]

你最好当心

那个戴亮星的男人

最好明白你是要去哪儿

或者原地不动

如果有天你到了那儿

---

[1] "如果有天你去休斯敦／小子，你最好乖乖走路"，引自美国民谣歌
手"铅肚皮"的歌曲《午夜专列》（"Midnight Special"），原曲改编
自囚歌。

[2] "巴格比和拉马尔"，可能指涉得克萨斯州历史博物馆，位于休斯敦
的巴格比街和拉马尔街交叉的街角上。

## On Bagby and Lamar

I know these streets
I've been here before
I nearly got killed here
During the Mexican war
Something always
Keeps me coming back for more
I know these streets
I've been here before

If you ever go to Dallas
Say hello to Mary Anne
Say I'm still pullin' on the trigger
Hangin' on the best that I can
If you see her sister Lucy
Say I'm sorry I'm not there
Tell her other sister Betsy
To pray the sinner's prayer

I got a restless fever
Burnin' in my brain
Got to keep ridin' forward
Can't spoil the game
The same way I leave here
Will be the way that I came

到了巴格比和拉马尔

我认识这些街
我以前来过
差点儿在这儿挂掉
在墨西哥战争时期
总是有些什么
让我一次次回来
我认识这些街
我以前来过


如果有天你去达拉斯
向玛丽·安妮问好
说我仍紧扣着扳机
尽我所能活下去
如果你见到她姐姐露西
说我很抱歉不能在那里
告诉另一个姐姐贝齐
要她去做悔罪祷告


我得了热病，辗转不宁
脑子里烧着
必须一直往前
不能再坏事儿
我怎么离开
就会怎么回来

Got a restless fever
Burnin' in my brain

If you ever go to Austin
Fort Worth or San Antone
Find the bar rooms I got lost in
And send my memories home
Put my tears in a bottle
Screw the top on tight
If you ever go to Houston
You better walk right

我得了热病，辗转不宁
脑子里烧着

如果有天你去奥斯汀
到沃思堡或者圣安东
去找一找我迷失的酒吧
把我的记忆带回家
把我的眼泪装进瓶子
拧紧盖子
如果有天你去休斯敦
你最好乖乖走路

## FORGETFUL HEART
(WITH ROBERT HUNTER)


Forgetful heart

Lost your power of recall

Every little detail

You don't remember at all

The times we knew

Who would remember better than you


Forgetful heart

We laughed and had a good time, you and I

It's been so long

Now you're content to let the days go by

When you were there

You were the answer to my prayer


Forgetful heart

We loved with all the love that life can give

What can I say

Without you it's so hard to live

Can't take much more

Why can't we love like we did before

## 健忘的心

（与罗伯特·亨特合作）

健忘的心
失去了回忆的能力
那每一个小细节
无从再记起
对我们相知的岁月
谁会比你记得更清晰

健忘的心
你和我，那美好时光，我们笑着
那已经是很久前
你现在满足于让一天天流过
只要你在那儿
就是我祈祷的应允

健忘的心
我们用生命能赐予的所有爱爱过了
我还能说什么
没有你日子难过
再也无法承受
为什么我们不能像从前一样相爱

Forgetful heart

Like a walking shadow in my brain

All night long

I lay awake and listen to the sound of pain

The door has closed forevermore

If indeed there ever was a door

健忘的心
就像我脑海中行走的暗影
整夜整夜
我醒着听那疼痛的声音
门永远关上了
如果真的，曾有一扇门

## JOLENE
(WITH ROBERT HUNTER)


Well you're comin' down High Street, walkin' in the sun
You make the dead man rise and holler she's the one
Jolene, Jolene
Baby, I am the king and you're the queen


Well it's a long old highway, don't ever end
I've got a Saturday night special, I'm back again
I'll sleep by your door, lay my life on the line
You probably don't know, but I'm gonna make you mine
Jolene, Jolene
Baby, I am the king and you're the queen


I keep my hands in my pocket, I'm movin' along
People think they know, but they're all wrong
You're something nice, I'm gonna grab my dice
If I can do it once, I can do it twice
Jolene, Jolene
Baby, I am the king and you're the queen


Well I found out the hard way, I've had my fill
You can't find somebody with his back to a hill

## 茱莲妮

（与罗伯特·亨特合作）


哦你沿繁华大街走来，走在阳光下
你让死人复活，大喊"她就是那一个"
茱莲妮，茱莲妮
宝贝啊，我是王，你是那王后


哦这漫长的老公路，没有尽头
我弄到一把"周六夜特用"，我回来了
我会睡你门口，赌上性命
你可能一无所知，但我会让你属于我
茱莲妮，茱莲妮
宝贝啊，我是王，你是那王后


我把手揣兜里，径直向前
人们以为知道，但他们都错了
你真是个尤物，我要抢过色子
只要让我做到一次，我就有第二次
茱莲妮，茱莲妮
宝贝啊，我是王，你是那王后


哦我知道这得来不易，对此我已尝透
你看不到那个人，他已没有退路

Those big brown eyes, they set off a spark

When you hold me in your arms things don't look so dark

Jolene, Jolene

Baby, I am the king and you're the queen

那褐色的大眼睛，放射出一道光焰
这时你搂着我，一切再不那么黑暗
茱莲妮，茱莲妮
宝贝啊，我是王，你是那王后

# THIS DREAM OF YOU

How long can I stay in this nowhere café
'Fore night turns into day
I wonder why I'm so frightened of dawn
All I have and all I know
Is this dream of you
Which keeps me living on

There's a moment when all old things
Become new again
But that moment might have been here and gone
All I have and all I know
Is this dream of you
Which keeps me living on

I look away, but I keep seeing it
I don't want to believe, but I keep believing it
Shadows dance upon the wall
Shadows that seem to know it all

Am I too blind to see?
Is my heart playing tricks on me?
Too late to stop now even though all my friends are gone

## 关于你的这个梦

在这乌有之乡的咖啡馆我还能待多久
当那黑夜尚未变成白昼
我在想为何我是如此害怕天明
所有我所有，所有我所知
是这个梦见你的梦
是它让我活下去

有这么一刻，所有的老朽
都再次新生
但是这一刻，想必来了又已失去
所有我所有，所有我所知
是这个梦见你的梦
是它让我活下去

我望向别处，可还是看见
我不想相信，却一直还在相信
影子们在墙上跳舞
那似乎什么都知道的影子

是我太瞎吗，所以瞧不见？
是我的心一直在耍我吗？
罢手已晚，纵使朋友们都已离去

All I have and all I know
Is this dream of you
Which keeps me living on

Everything I touch seems to disappear
Everywhere I turn you are always here
I'll run this race until my earthly death
I'll defend this place with my dying breath

From a cheerless room in a curtained gloom
I saw a star from heaven fall
I turned and looked again but it was gone
All I have and all I know
Is this dream of you
Which keeps me living on

所有我所有，所有我所知
是这个梦见你的梦
是它让我活下去

我手触到的一切，似乎在消逝
无论我转向哪里，你一直都在这里
我将继续这场赛跑直到尘世生命终结
我将保卫这地方用我那垂死的呼吸

从帘幕沉沉的郁闷房间
我看见一颗星从天上坠落
等我转头再看，它已消失不见
所有我所有，所有我所知
是这个梦见你的梦
是它让我活下去

## SHAKE SHAKE MAMA
### (WITH ROBERT HUNTER)


I get the blues for you baby when I look up at the sun
I get the blues for you baby when I look up at the sun
Come back here we can have some real fun

Well it's early in the evening and everything is still
Well it's early in the evening and everything is still
One more time, I'm walking up on Heartbreak Hill

Shake, shake mama, like a ship goin' out to sea
Shake, shake mama, like a ship goin' out to sea
You took all my money and you give it to Richard Lee

Down by the river Judge Simpson walkin' around
Down by the river Judge Simpson walkin' around
Nothing shocks me more than that old clown

Some of you women you really know your stuff
Some of you women you really know your stuff

## 摇啊摇啊妈妈
（与罗伯特·亨特合作）


你让我郁郁不乐宝贝当我抬头看太阳
你让我郁郁不乐宝贝当我抬头看太阳
回到这儿来吧我们来真正地乐一场

哦入夜还不久一切都很平静
哦入夜还不久一切都很平静
再一次，我在攀登那心碎山的山顶

摇啊摇啊妈妈，像一艘船要出海去
摇啊摇啊妈妈，像一艘船要出海去
你拿光我的钱把它全给了理查德·李

沿着河岸辛普森法官在踱步
沿着河岸辛普森法官在踱步
没谁比那个老小丑，更让我震惊不已 [1]

有些女人你们真的搞明白了自己的东西
有些女人你们真的搞明白了自己的东西

---

[1] "没谁比那个老小丑，更让我震惊不已"，引自戴维·赖特译乔叟小
说《坎特伯雷故事》"法庭差役的故事"篇。

But your clothes are all torn and your language is a little
  too rough

Shake, shake mama, shake it 'til the break of day
Shake, shake mama, shake it 'til the break of day
I'm right here baby, I'm not that far away

I'm motherless, fatherless, almost friendless too
I'm motherless, fatherless, almost friendless too
It's Friday morning on Franklin Avenue

Shake, shake mama, raise your voice and pray
Shake, shake mama, raise your voice and pray
If you're goin' on home, better go the shortest way

但你们的衣服都破了你们的语言有点儿
　粗鄙


摇啊摇啊妈妈，摇啊直到天破晓
摇啊摇啊妈妈，摇啊直到天破晓
我就在这儿宝贝，我并没有走掉


我无母、无父，也几乎无朋友
我无母、无父，也几乎无朋友 [1]
这是星期五的早晨在富兰克林大道


摇啊摇啊妈妈，提高嗓门儿祈祷
摇啊摇啊妈妈，提高嗓门儿祈祷
如果你要回家，最好抄最近的道


---

[1] "我无母、无父，也几乎无朋友"，源自美国蓝调与爵士歌手朗尼·约
　翰逊（Lonnie Johnson）的《无朋友又忧郁》（"Friendless and Blue",
　1938）："我无母我无父，我也几乎无朋友。"

# I FEEL A CHANGE COMIN' ON
(WITH ROBERT HUNTER)


Well I'm looking the world over

Looking far off into the East

And I see my baby coming

She's walking with the village priest

I feel a change coming on

And the last part of the day is already gone


We got so much in common

We strive for the same old ends

And I just can't wait

Wait for us to become friends

I feel a change coming on

And the fourth part of the day is already gone


Life is for love

And they say that love is blind

If you want to live easy

Baby pack your clothes with mine

## 我感到一个变化在临近

（与罗伯特·亨特合作）


哦我望遍世界

远望到东方

望见我的小宝贝

和村里的神父一起走来

我感到一个变化在临近

而这一天的最后一部分业已过去


我们有这么多相同之处

我们争取着一样的结局

而我已等不及

等不及我们成为朋友

我感到一个变化在临近

而这一天的第四个部分业已过去 [1]


人生是为了爱

而他们说爱是盲目的

如果你想活得轻松

宝贝把你的衣服和我的收拾在一起

---

[1] "而这一天的第四个部分业已过去"，源自戴维·赖特译乔叟小说《坎特伯雷故事》"律师的故事"篇。

I feel a change coming on
And the fourth part of the day is already gone

Ain't no use in dreamin'
I got better things to do
Dreams never worked anyway
Even when they did come true

You're as whorish as ever
It ain't no surprise
We see the meaning of life
In each other's eyes
I feel a change coming on
And the fourth part of the day is already gone

I'm hearing Billy Joe Shaver
And I'm reading James Joyce
Some people they tell me
I got the blood of the land in my voice

Everybody got all the money
Everybody got all the beautiful clothes
Everybody got all the flowers

我感到一个变化在临近
而这一天的第四个部分业已过去

做梦没什么用
我有更该做的事
做梦从不起作用
哪怕它们真的变成真的

你一如既往地妖冶
这并不令人惊讶
我们看见生活的意义
就在彼此的眼睛里
我感到一个变化在临近
而这一天的第四个部分业已过去

我听着比利·乔·谢弗 [1]
我读着詹姆斯·乔伊斯
有一些人告诉我
我的声音里有土地的血

人人有了钱
人人有了漂亮衣服
人人有了花

---

[1] 比利·乔·谢弗（Billy Joe Shaver, 1939—2020），得克萨斯乡村音乐歌手和词作者。

I don't have one single rose

I feel a change coming on

And the fourth part of the day is already gone

我甚至没有一枝玫瑰
我感到一个变化在临近
而这一天的第四个部分业已过去

## IT'S ALL GOOD
(WITH ROBERT HUNTER)

Talk about me babe, if you must

Throw on the dirt, pile on the dust

I'd do the same thing if I could

You've heard what they say—they say it's all good

All good

It's all good

Big politician telling lies

Restaurant kitchen, all full of flies

Don't make a bit of difference, don't see why it should

I'll tell ya somethin'—it's all good

It's all good

It's all good

Wives are leavin' their husbands, they beginning to roam

They leave the party and they never get home

I wouldn't change it, even if I could

Same ol' story—it's all good

It's all good

All good

## 一切都好

（与罗伯特·亨特合作）


议论我吧宝贝，如果你必须
扔来泥巴，堆起尘灰
如果我可以我也会这么干
你听见他们说了——他们说一切都好
都好
一切都好


大政客在说谎
餐馆厨房里，全是苍蝇
千万别作区分，别弄懂为何这样
我会告诉你一点——一切都好
一切都好
一切都好


妻子们离开丈夫，开始转悠
就是聚会散了也决不回家
我不会做改变，纵使我能做改变
还是老一套——一切都好
一切都好
都好

Brick by brick, they tear you down
A teacup of water is enough to drown
Check your oil, look under the hood
Whatever you see, it's all good
All good
Say it's all good

People in the country, people on the land
Some so sick, they can hardly stand
Everybody would move away, if they could
It's hard to believe but it's all good
Yeah

The widow's cry, the orphan's plea
Everywhere you look, more misery
Come 'long with me, babe, I wish you would
You know what I'm sayin', it's all good
All good, I said it's all good
All good

Cold blooded killer, stalking the town
Cop cars blinking, something bad going down
Buildings are crumbling in the neighborhood
No doubt about it, it's all good
It's all good
They say it's all good

一块接一块，他们把你拆掉
一杯水足以淹死人
去检查燃油，看看引擎盖下
不管看到什么，一切都好
都好
说一切都好

这国家的人，这土地上的人
有的已如此崩溃，就快要撑不住
每个人都想离开，假使他可以
这难以置信，但一切都好
是的

寡妇的哭喊，孤儿的求乞
你望向各处，看到更多痛苦
跟我来宝贝，我希望你乐意
你知道我要说什么，一切都好
都好，我说一切都好
都好

冷血凶手，城中游荡
警灯闪耀，罪案滋长
邻近的建筑物在崩塌
别怀疑，一切都好
一切都好
他们说一切都好

I'll pluck off your beard and blow it in your face

This time tomorrow I'll be rolling in your place

I'm going out back, get some firewood

It is what it is, and it's all good

It's all good

我将拔下你的胡须吹你脸上
明天这时候我将睡在你的地方
我出去一下就回，弄一些柴火
就是这样，而一切都好
一切都好

# ROUGH
# AND
# ROWDY
# WAYS

# ROUGH AND ROWDY WAYS
# 粗野风格

2020 年 6 月 19 日，哥伦比亚唱片公司发行了鲍勃·迪伦第 39 张录音室专辑《粗野风格》。

这一年，一场传播极为广泛的传染病正席卷全球，众多公共事务停摆。

这一年，迪伦 79 岁，像他的"永不停止的巡演"所宣称的，他的工作没有停摆。《粗野风格》的最后一曲《最卑鄙的谋杀》，是他唱过的最长的歌曲，16 分 54 秒，在双张唱片中占了整整一面，英文有 1548 个单词，翻译成中文足有 2200 余字。

在这首歌中，迪伦唱了 1963 年 11 月肯尼迪总统在达拉斯遇刺的事件：他被子弹爆头，一命归西。在这首歌末尾，迪伦为所有相关者和不相关者，为"我"和"我们"，为没有主人的狗，播放了可能是他一生中最喜欢的歌，也包括这首《最卑鄙的谋杀》。这些歌仿佛构成了一部美国史，民间的、传说的、隐秘流传的，就像他自己的吟唱生涯。

这令人联想起迪伦的上一张全原创专辑《暴风雨》，在该专辑末尾，他也唱了一首超长歌曲，唱给"泰坦尼克号"的 1600 多个亡灵。然而，虽然二者在多方面极为相像，但《粗野风格》与《暴风雨》立意完全不同。

事实上，在这张专辑中迪伦仿佛忘记了死亡，忘记了他的高龄。《粗野风格》视野敞开，更向着生路、更兴奋，迪伦眼中所见并不是葬礼，而是这片云海翻腾的世界。

在这张专辑之前，迪伦制作发行了他的第36、37和38张录音室专辑，2015年的《夜之阴影》（*Shadows in the Night*），2016年的《堕落天使》（*Fallen Angels*），2017年的《一式三份》（*Triplicate*）。与以往专注于老民歌的翻唱不同，这3张翻唱专辑涵盖了众多经典流行歌曲，并从中修炼出一种炉火纯青的，更深厚、更典雅、更平正的，更像是老歌唱家的歌唱。现在，他把这种歌唱带到了《粗野风格》专辑。

10首歌曲，俱由"永不停止的巡演"原班人马，搭配上临时乐手，于2020年1月至3月初在洛杉矶的音城录音室完成。专辑仍是老美国风扑面，然而，这次有令人难以置信的音乐多样性。

我觉得，理解这些歌曲不是要向后看，而是要往前看。尽管迪伦一开口，就会拖曳起岁月的尘烟、历史的重重暗影，以及来自《圣经》、神话、文学典籍和老民歌的密集典故，但是这张专辑并不是一辑挽歌。

《我包含众多》引用了惠特曼的诗歌，也兼具惠特曼开拓进取和包罗万象的精神。当然，它是迪伦一生的总结，但这样的一生，也还在继续展开。这歌曲向着死，可也明确向着生，"我与生和死同床共眠"，"我走到所有东西都失去——又重新变好的地方"。

"我向世界敞开我心，世界进来了"——《假先知》，也有这种向外敞开的博大，由此迪伦为自己一生的创作正名，"我不是假先知——我只知道我知道的"。而看他的表情，豪情万丈，仍在信心百倍地出手，与反基督者和"黑骑士"作战，要拿剑砍掉他们的手臂，"我是没有活过的、无意义生活的敌人"。

他还想动用弗兰肯斯坦之术，组装一个《我自己版本的你》，这首歌也是向前、是进取的，仍在雄心勃勃地要大干一场，以实践他在40岁前后领悟的主张。紧接着的《我已下定决心把自己给你》，可以当作给所爱之人的火炬情歌，也完全可以理解为：这忠贞不渝的对象是信念。《再见吉米·里德》也是如此，这位"成不了大器"的布鲁斯乐手、传教士，却是迪伦眼中最伟大的。他对里德说的话，也是夫子自道。

他呼唤《缪斯之母》，祈请她创造伟大的艺术。他《越过卢比孔河》，要迎接最艰巨的决战。《基韦斯特（哲学家海盗）》又是一部音乐史、诗歌史、个人史的集合，以迪伦神秘的"杂耍乱炖"方式写就，表明了要继续在这条路上走下去。甚至《最卑鄙的谋杀》，现在你看清了吧，它不是葬礼进行曲，而是属灵战争[1]的一幕，而战斗仍在继续。

这是一场漫长而壮丽的远征。并不十分自觉，迪伦在恍惚状态下为这个剧烈动荡的世界插上了他的"定海神针"。2012年，迪伦曾表露，他打心眼儿里想再写一些宗教歌曲，作为"基督教三部曲"的延续。我觉得，这张唱片就是。

---

[1]《圣经》中的概念，是指信徒在信仰生活中所面临的来自魔鬼、罪恶和世俗诱惑的斗争。——编者注

# I CONTAIN MULTITUDES

Today and tomorrow and yesterday too
The flowers are dying like all things do
Follow me close—I'm going to Bally-Na-Lee
I'll lose my mind if you don't come with me
I fuss with my hair and I fight blood feuds . . . I contain
   multitudes

Gotta tell tale heart like Mr. Poe
Got skeletons in the walls of people you know
I'll drink to the truth of things that we said
I'll drink to the man that shares your bed
I paint landscapes—I paint nudes. . . I contain multitudes

A red Cadillac and a black moustache

# 我包含众多 [1]

今天和明天还有昨天

花儿在死去就像一切

跟紧我——我要去巴利纳利 [2]

你要是不跟我来我会疯掉

我拨弄头发，我抗击血仇……我包含

众多

有泄密的心像坡先生 [3] 一样

你认识的人他们的骷髅在墙里

我会为那些事情的真相干杯

我会为和你同床的男人干杯

我画风景——我画裸体……我包含众多

红色凯迪拉克和黑胡子 [4]

---

[1] 歌名典出沃尔特·惠特曼的诗歌《我自己之歌》（"Song of Myself"）中的诗句："我自相矛盾吗？／那好吧，我就是自相矛盾，／我宽广博大，我包含众多。"

[2] 爱尔兰北部小镇。典出莱夫特利（Antoine ó Raifteiri）的诗歌《巴利纳利的姑娘》（"The Lass from Bally-na-Lee"）。

[3] 指美国作家埃德加·爱伦·坡（Edgar Allan Poe），《泄密的心》是他的一篇短篇小说。本首歌后面的内容也与坡的小说有关。

[4] 《红色凯迪拉克和黑胡子》（"Red Cadillac and a Black Mustache"）是沃伦·史密斯（Warren Smith）的歌曲。

Rings on my fingers that sparkle and flash
Tell me what's next—what shall we do
Half my soul baby belongs to you
I rollick and I frolic with all the young dudes. . . I contain
multitudes

I'm just like Anne Frank—like Indiana Jones
And them British bad boys the Rolling Stones
I go right to the edge—I go right to the end
I go right where all things lost—are made good again

I sing the songs of experience like William Blake
I have no apologies to make
Everything's flowin' all at the same time
I live on the boulevard of crime
I drive fast cars and I eat fast foods . . . I contain multitudes

我手指上闪闪发光的戒指

告诉我接下来是什么——我们该怎么做

我一半的灵魂属于你宝贝

我和那些小伙子嬉戏玩耍 [1]……我包含

众多


我就像安妮·弗兰克 [2]——就像印第安纳·琼斯 [3]

还有他们滚石乐队的英国坏男孩

我一直走到边缘——我一直走到尽头

我走到所有东西都失去——又重新变好的地方


我像威廉·布莱克一样唱经验之歌 [4]

我不需要道歉什么

一切都在同一时刻流动

我住在犯罪大道

我开快车，我吃快餐……我包含众多

---

[1] 参见大卫·鲍伊（David Bowie）的歌曲《所有年轻人》（"All the Young Dudes"）。

[2] 安妮·弗兰克（Anne Frank），生于德国的荷兰犹太人，13 岁时开始创作《安妮日记》，纳粹大屠杀中最著名的受害者之一。

[3] 小亨利·沃尔顿·"印第安纳"·琼斯博士（Dr. Henry Walton "Indiana" Jones, Jr.），出自系列冒险电影《夺宝奇兵》（*Indiana Jones*），典型形象为哈里森·福特（Harrison Ford）所扮演的牛仔装扮的人物。

[4] 指《经验之歌》（*Songs of Experience*），英国浪漫主义诗人威廉·布莱克（William Blake）的作品。

Pink pedal pushers and red blue jeans
All the pretty maids and all the old queens
All the old queens from all my past lives
I carry four pistols and two large knives
I'm a man of contradictions and a man of many moods . . . I
  contain multitudes

Greedy old wolf—I'll show you my heart
But not all of it—only the hateful part
I'll sell you down the river—I'll put a price on your head
What more can I tell ya—I sleep with life and death
  in the same bed

Get lost Madam—get up off my knee
Keep your mouth away from me
I'll keep the path open—the path in my mind
I'll see to it that there's no love left behind
I play Beethoven sonatas Chopin's preludes . . . I contain
  multitudes

粉色七分裤 [1] 和红色牛仔裤

所有漂亮的女仆和所有老女王

来自我前世的所有老女王

我带着四支手枪和两把大刀

我自相矛盾，我情绪多变……我包含

　　众多


贪婪的老狼 [2]——我会给你看我的心

但不是全部——只是可恨的那部分

我会把你卖到河边——我会在你的头上标上价格

我还能告诉你什么——我与生和死

　　同床共眠


走吧女士——从我的膝盖上站起来

让你的嘴远离我 [3]

我会保持道路敞开——我心中的道路

我会确保没有任何爱留下

我弹贝多芬奏鸣曲肖邦前奏曲……我包含

　　众多

---

[1]　参见美国摇滚先驱卡尔·帕金斯（Carl Perkins）1958 年发行的同名
　　　歌曲。

[2]　参见爱伦·坡《泄密的心》（"The Tell-Tale Heart"）等几篇短篇小说。

[3]　参见 17 世纪爱尔兰诗歌《把你的吻留给自己》（"Keep Your Kiss to
　　　Yourself"）。

# FALSE PROPHET

Another day without end—another ship going out
Another day of anger—bitterness and doubt
I know how it happened—I saw it begin
I opened my heart to the world and the world came in

Hello Mary Lou—Hello Miss Pearl
My fleet footed guides from the underworld
No stars in the sky shine brighter than you
You girls mean business and I do too

I'm the enemy of treason—the enemy of strife
I'm the enemy of the unlived meaningless life
I ain't no false prophet—I just know what I know
I go where only the lonely can go

# 假先知

又一天没有尽头——又一艘船驶离港口
又一天满是愤怒——苦涩还有怀疑
我知道如何发生——我看到如何开始
我向世界敞开我心，世界进来了


你好玛丽·露 [1]——你好珍珠小姐 [2]
我来自地下的疾行向导
天上没有星星比你更亮
姑娘你们是认真的，我也一样


我是叛国的敌人——纷争的敌人
我是没有活过的无意义生活的敌人
我不是假先知——我只知道我知道的
我去只有孤独的人可以去的地方 [3]

---

[1] 《你好玛丽·露》（"Hello Mary Lou"）是美国音乐家吉尼·皮特尼（Gene
Pitney）创作的歌曲，1960 年由约翰尼·邓肯（Johnny Duncan）首次
录制。

[2] 《珍珠小姐》（"Miss Pearl"）是吉米·威奇斯（Jimmy Wages）的一
首歌曲。也参见但丁《神曲》中贝雅特丽齐的典故。

[3] 《只有孤独的人》（"Only the Lonely"）是罗伊·奥比森（Roy Orbison）
的一首歌曲。

I'm first among equals—second to none
I'm last of the best—you can bury the rest
Bury 'em naked with their silver and gold
Put 'em six feet under and then pray for their souls

What are you lookin' at—there's nothing to see
Just a cool breeze encircling me
Let's walk in the garden—so far and so wide
We can sit in the shade by the fountain side

I've searched the world over for the Holy Grail
I sing songs of love—I sing songs of betrayal
Don't care what I drink—don't care what I eat
I climbed a mountain of swords on my bare feet

You don't know me darlin'—you never would guess
I'm nothing like my ghostly appearance would suggest
I ain't no false prophet—I just said what I said
I'm here to bring vengeance on somebody's head

Put out your hand—there's nothin' to hold
Open your mouth—I'll stuff it with gold
Oh you poor Devil—look up if you will
The City of God is there on the hill

Hello stranger—Hello and goodbye

我是同类中的第一名——无人可比
我是最好中的最后一个——你可以埋葬剩下的
用他们的金银埋葬赤裸的他们
把他们埋在六英尺以下，再为他们的灵魂祈祷


你在看什么呢——没什么可看的
只是一阵凉风环绕着我
让我们在花园里走走——那么远，那么宽
我们可以坐在喷泉边的阴凉里


我在整个世界寻找圣杯
我唱着爱之歌——我唱着背叛之歌
不在乎喝什么——不在乎吃什么
我光着脚上了一座刀山


你不了解我，亲爱的——你永远猜不到
我不像我幽灵般的外表那样
我不是假先知——我只是说了我说的话
我来这里是为了把报复带到某人头上


伸出你的手——没有什么可抓的
张开你的嘴——我会用金子把它塞满
哦，你这可怜的魔鬼——假如你愿意的话，抬头看看
上帝之城就在山上


你好，陌生人——你好，再见

You rule the land but so do I

You lusty old mule—you got a poisoned brain

I'm gonna marry you to a ball and chain


You know darlin' the kind of life that I live

When your smile meets my smile—something's got to give

I ain't no false prophet—I'm nobody's bride

Can't remember when I was born and I forgot when I died

你统治这片土地，但我也一样
你这精力充沛的老骡子——你的大脑中毒了
我要让你和枷锁结为夫妻

你知道，亲爱的，我过着怎样的生活
当你的微笑遇见我的微笑——有些事情必须发生
我不是假先知——我不是谁的新娘
不记得我什么时候出生，也忘了我什么时候死去

# MY OWN VERSION OF YOU

All through the summers and into January
I've been visiting morgues and monasteries
Looking for the necessary body parts
Limbs and livers and brains and hearts

I want to bring someone to life—is what I want to do
I want to create my own version of you

It must be the winter of my discontent
I wish you'd taken me with you wherever you went
They talk all night—they talk all day
Not for a second do I believe what they say

I want to bring someone to life—someone I've never seen
You know what I mean—you know exactly what I mean

## 我自己版本的你 [1]

整个夏天直到一月
我都在去停尸房和修道院
寻找必要的身体部位
四肢，肝脏，大脑，心脏

我想让一个人复活——这是我想做的事
我想造一个我自己版本的你

这一定是我寒冬一样的宿怨 [2]
我希望你无论走到哪里都带着我
他们整晚都在说话——他们整天都在说话
我一刻也不相信他们所说的

我想让一个人复活——一个我从未见过的人
你知道我的意思——你完全明白我的意思

---

[1] 参见玛丽·雪莱（Mary Shelley）的小说《弗兰肯斯坦》（*Frankenstein*）。
[2] 典出莎士比亚历史剧《理查三世》（*Richard III*）："现在我们那像
寒冬一样的宿怨已给这颗约克的太阳融化成为壮美的夏天；那笼罩
着我们王室的片片乌云已全都埋进了海洋的深渊。"（"Now is the
winter of our discontent/ Made glorious summer by this sun of York;/
And all the clouds that lour'd upon our house / In the deep bosom of
the ocean buried." ）

I'll take Scarface Pacino and the Godfather Brando
Mix 'em up in a tank and get a robot commando
If I do it upright and put the head on straight
I'll be saved by the creature that I create
I get blood from a cactus—make gunpowder from ice
I don't gamble with cards and I don't shoot no dice
Can you look in my face with your sightless eye
Can you cross your heart and hope to die

I'll bring someone to life—someone for real
Someone who feels the way that I feel

I study Sanskrit and Arabic to improve my mind
I want to do things for the benefit of all mankind
I say to the willow tree—don't weep for me
I'm saying the hell with all things that used to be
I get into trouble and I hit the wall
No place to turn—no place at all
I pick a number between one and two
And I ask myself what would Julius Caesar do

我要用疤面人帕西诺和教父白兰度 [1]

将他们混合在水箱中，再来个机器人突击队长 [2]

如果我弄得够好，把头也正正地装上

我会被我创造的生命所拯救

我从仙人掌中取血——用冰做火药

我不赌牌也不掷骰子

你能用你看不见的眼睛看着我的脸吗

你能对天发誓吗


我会让一个人复活——真正地复活

一个有我一样感觉的人


我学习梵文和阿拉伯文，为了训练思维

我要为全人类的利益而工作

我对柳树说——不要为我哭泣

我是说滚吧所有过去的事情

我遇到了麻烦，我筋疲力尽

无处可去——根本无处可去

我在一和二之间挑了一个数字

我问自己，尤利乌斯·恺撒会怎么做

---

[1]  阿尔·帕西诺（Al Pacino）曾出演电影《疤面人》（*Scarface*）。马龙·白
     兰度（Marlon Brando）曾出演电影《教父》（*The Godfather*）。

[2]  《机器人突击队长》（*Robot Commando*）是一部 1986 年出版的美
     国科幻漫画。

I'll bring someone to life—in more ways than one
Don't matter how long it takes—it'll be done when it's done

I'm gonna make you play the piano like Leon Russell
Like Liberace—like St. John the Apostle
Play every number that I can play
I'll see you baby on Judgement Day
After midnight if you still want to meet
I'll be at the Black Horse Tavern on Armageddon Street
Two doors down not that far to walk
I'll hear your footsteps—you won't have to knock

I'll bring someone to life—balance the scales
I'm not gonna get involved in any insignificant details

You can bring it to St. Peter—you can bring it to Jerome
You can move it on over—bring it all the way home
Bring it to the corner where the children play
You can bring it to me on a silver tray

我会让一个人复活——以不止一种方式

不管需要多长时间——完成后就会完成


我会让你像利昂·拉塞尔 [1] 一样弹钢琴

像李伯拉斯 [2]——像使徒约翰

弹我能弹的每一首曲子

我会在审判日见到你，宝贝

午夜过后如果你还想见面

我会在世界末日街的黑马酒馆

要走过两扇门并不远

我会听到你的脚步声——你不必敲门


我会让一个人复活——平衡天平

我不会卷入任何无关的细节


你可以把它带给圣彼得——你可以把它带给杰罗姆 [3]

你可以把它带过来——一直带回家

把它带到孩子们玩耍的角落

你可以用银托盘把它拿给我


---

[1] 利昂·拉塞尔（Leon Russell），美国音乐家，创作了大量畅销唱片。

[2] 李伯拉斯（Władziu Valentino Liberace），美国钢琴家、歌手、演员。

[3] 典出美国吉他演奏家波·迪德利（Bo Diddley）的曲目《把它带给杰罗姆》（"Bring It to Jerome"）。

I'll bring someone to life—spare no expense

Do it with decency and common sense

Can you tell me what it means to be or not to be

You won't get away with fooling me

Can you help me walk that moonlight mile

Can you give me the blessings of your smile

I want to bring someone to life—use all my powers

Do it in the dark in the wee small hours

I can see the history of the whole human race

It's all right there—its carved into your face

Should I break it all down—should I fall on my knees

Is there light at the end of the tunnel—can you tell me please

Stand over there by the Cypress tree

Where the Trojan women and children were sold into slavery

Long ago before the First Crusade

Way back before England or America were made

Step right into the burning hell

Where some of the best known enemies of mankind dwell

我会让某人复活——不惜一切代价

过程中带着操守和常识

你能告诉我生存还是毁灭意味着什么吗 [1]

你根本就骗不了我

你能帮我走月光下的一英里吗 [2]

你能给我你微笑的祝福吗

我想让某人复活——用我全部的力量

在黎明前的黑暗时刻

我可以看到整个人类的历史

全都在那里——刻在你的脸上

我应该把这一切都打碎吗——我应该跪下吗

隧道尽头有光吗——你能告诉我吗

站在那边的柏树旁

特洛伊妇女和儿童被卖为奴隶的地方

很久以前在第一次"十字军"东征之前

早在英格兰或美利坚诞生之前

步入燃烧的地狱

人类最著名的那些敌人居住的地方

---

[1] 典出莎士比亚《哈姆雷特》(*Hamlet*)第三幕第一场:"生存还是
    毁灭,这是一个值得考虑的问题。"("To be, or not to be, that is the
    question.")

[2] 典出滚石乐队(The Rolling Stones)1971 年的歌曲《月光下的一英
    里》("Moonlight Mile")。

Mister Freud with his dreams and Mister Marx with his axe

See the raw hide lash rip the skin off their backs

You got the right spirit—you can feel it you can hear it

You got what they call the immortal spirit

You can feel it all night you can feel it in the morn

Creeps into your body the day you are born

One strike of lightning is all that I need

And a blast of 'lectricity that runs at top speed

Show me your ribs—I'll stick in the knife

I'm gonna jump start my creation to life


I want to bring someone to life—turn back the years

Do it with laughter—do it with tears

弗洛伊德先生带着他的梦，马克思先生带着他的斧头

看到皮鞭从他们背上撕下皮肤

你有正确的灵魂——你能感觉到你能听得到

你有他们所谓的不朽灵魂

整晚都能感觉到，早上也能感觉到

在你出生的那一天悄悄进入你的身体

我只需要一击闪电

还有以最快速度运行的电流

给我看看你的肋骨——我会插一把刀

我要给我的创造开启生命


我要让一个人复活——让时光倒流

用笑声——用泪水

# I'VE MADE UP MY MIND TO GIVE MYSELF TO YOU

Sitting on my terrace lost in the stars
Listenin' to the sounds of the sad guitars
Been thinking it over and I thought it all through
I've made up my mind to give myself to you

I saw the first fall of snow
I saw the flowers come and go
I don't think anyone else ever knew
I made up my mind to give myself to you

I'm giving myself to you, I am
From Salt Lake City to Birmingham
From East L.A. to San Antone
I don't think I could bear to live my life alone

My eye is like a shooting star
It looks at nothing, neither near or far
No one ever told me, it's just something I knew
I've made up my mind to give myself to you

## 我已下定决心把自己给你

坐在露台上迷失在星空里
聆听悲伤吉他的声音
一直在思考，想了很久
我已下定决心把自己给你

我看见第一场雪落下
我看见花儿来了又去
我想别人都不知道
我已下定决心把自己给你

我会把自己给你，我会
从盐湖城到伯明翰
从东洛杉矶到圣安东 [1]
我不认为我能忍受一个人的生活

我的眼睛像流星
什么也不看，无论近或是远
从没有人告诉我，我只是知道
我已下定决心把自己给你

---

[1] 美国得克萨斯州城市圣安东尼奥（San Antonio）。

If I had the wings of a snow white dove
I'd preach the gospel, the gospel of love
A love so real—a love so true
I made up my mind to give myself to you

Take me out traveling, you're a traveling man
Show me something that I'll understand
I'm not what I was, things aren't what they were
I'm going to go far away from home with her

I traveled the long road of despair
I met no other traveler there
A lot of people gone, a lot of people I knew
I've made up my mind to give myself to you

My heart's like a river—a river that sings
It just takes me a while to realize things
I'll see you at sunrise—I'll see you at dawn
I'll lay down beside you, when everyone is gone

From the plains and the prairies—from the mountains to the sea
I hope that the gods go easy with me
I knew you'd say yes—I'm saying it too
I've made up my mind to give myself to you

假如我有翅膀像雪白鸽子
我要传福音，爱的福音
如此真切的爱——如此真实的爱
我已下定决心把自己给你

带我去旅行，你是个旅行的人
让我看见那我能理解的事
我不是原来的我，事情不是原来的样子
我要和她一起远离家乡

我走过了漫长的绝望之路
我没有遇到其他旅行者
很多人走了，很多人我认识
我已下定决心把自己给你

我的心像一条河——一条会歌唱的河
只是需要一段时间才能理解事情
我会在日出时见到你——我会在黎明时见到你
我会在你身边躺下，当所有人都走了以后

从平原和草原——从高山到大海
我希望神灵能温柔待我
我知道你会说是的——我也这么说
我已下定决心把自己给你

## BLACK RIDER

Black Rider Black Rider you been livin' too hard
You been up all night havin' to stay on your guard
The path that you're walkin'—is too narrow to walk
Every step of the way another stumblin' block
The road that you're on—same road that you know
But it's not the same as—it was a minute ago

Black Rider Black Rider you've seen it all
You've seen the great world and you've seen the small
You fell into the fire and you're eating the flame
Better seal up your lips if you want to stay in the game
Be reasonable Mister—be honest be fair
Let all of your earthly thoughts be a prayer

Black Rider Black Rider all dressed in black
I'm walking away and you try to make me look back
My heart is at rest I'd like to keep it that way
I don't want to fight—at least not today
Go home to your wife stop visiting mine
One of these days I'll forget to be kind

Black Rider Black Rider tell me when—tell me how

## 黑骑士

黑骑士黑骑士你活得太辛苦

你彻夜未眠不得不保持警醒

你走的路——太窄了

每一步都是新的绊脚石

你正在走的路——你认得的同一条路

但这路不同——和一分钟前不一样


黑骑士黑骑士你什么都看过

你看到了伟大的世界，也看到了渺小的世界

你掉进火里吃着火焰

如果你想留在游戏中，最好闭上你的嘴

清醒一点先生——诚实一点公正一点

让你的世俗想法全都成为祈祷


黑骑士黑骑士一身黑衣

我已经走开而你试图让我回头看

我的心已安息，我想一直保持

我不想战斗——至少今天不想

回家找你老婆别再来找我

有一天我会忘记要做个好人


黑骑士黑骑士告诉我什么时候——告诉我怎么做

If there ever was a time then let it be now
Let me go through—open the door
My soul is distressed my mind is at war
Don't hug me—don't flatter me—don't turn on the charm
I'll take out a sword and have to hack off your arm

Black Rider Black Rider hold it right there
The size of your cock will get you nowhere
I'll suffer in silence I'll not make a sound
Maybe I'll take the—high moral ground
Some enchanted evening I'll sing you a song
Black Rider Black Rider you've been on the job too long

如果曾经有过那么就让它成为现在
让我过去——把门打开
我的灵魂很苦恼我的心在争战
不要拥抱我——不要恭维我——不要施展魅力
我会拿出一把剑砍掉你的手臂

黑骑士黑骑士站住别动
你那玩意儿的大小其实毫无作用
我会默默忍受我不会发出声音
也许我会占据——道德高地
着魔的夜晚，我会为你唱歌
黑骑士黑骑士你工作太久了

# GOODBYE JIMMY REED

I live on a street named after a Saint
Women in the churches wear powder and paint
Where the Jews and the Catholics and the Muslims all pray
I can tell a Proddy from a mile away
Goodbye Jimmy Reed—Jimmy Reed indeed
Give me that old time religion, it's just what I need

For thine is the kingdom, the power and the glory
Go tell it on the Mountain, go tell the real story
Tell it in that straight forward puritanical tone
In the mystic hours when a person's alone
Goodbye Jimmy Reed—Godspeed
Thump on the bible—proclaim the creed

You won't amount to much the people all said
'Cause I didn't play guitar behind my head
Never pandered never acted proud

## 再见吉米·里德 [1]

我住在一条以圣徒命名的街上
每个教堂里的女人都涂脂抹粉
犹太人天主教徒和穆斯林都在那里祈祷
我可以从一英里外认出一个新教徒
再见吉米·里德——真的，吉米·里德
给我那个旧日的信仰 [2]，这正是我所需要的

因为国度、权柄和荣耀全是你的
到山岭上传扬 [3]，传扬真实的故事
用那种直截了当的清教徒语气
在一个人孤单的神秘时刻
再见吉米·里德——路平安
敲打圣经——宣讲信条

你成不了大器，人们都那么说
因为我没有在脑后弹吉他
从不讨好从不骄傲

---

[1]  吉米·里德（Jimmy Reed），美国布鲁斯音乐家。

[2]  《给我那个旧日信仰》（"Give Me That Old-Time Religion"）是 19 世纪的一首著名福音歌曲。

[3]  《到山岭上传扬》（"Go Tell It on the Mountain"）是一首著名美国黑人灵歌。

Never took off my shoes and threw them into the crowd
Goodbye Jimmy Reed—goodbye and goodnight
I'll put a jewel in your crown—I'll put out the light

They threw everything at me, everything in the book
Had nothing to fight with but a butcher's hook
They have no pity—they don't lend a hand
And I can't sing a song that I don't understand
Goodbye Jimmy Reed—goodbye and good luck
Can't play the record 'cause my needle got stuck

Transparent woman in a transparent dress
It suits you well—I must confess
I'll break open your grapes I'll suck out the juice
I need you like my head needs a noose
Goodbye Jimmy Reed, goodbye and so long
I thought I could resist her but I was so wrong

G-d be with you, brother dear
If you don't mind me asking, what brings you here?
Oh, nothing much, I'm just looking for the man
I came to see where he's lying in this lost land
Goodbye Jimmy Reed and with everything within ya
Can't you hear me calling from down in Virginia

从不脱鞋扔进人群

再见吉米·里德——再见，晚安

我会在你的王冠上镶一颗宝石——我会熄灭光芒


他们把一切都扔向我，书中的一切

没有什么武器，除了屠夫的钩子

他们没有怜悯——他们不会伸手

我无法唱我所不懂的歌

再见吉米·里德——再见，祝你好运

无法播放唱片，因为唱针卡住了


穿透明衣服的透明女人

很适合你——我必须承认

我会打开你的葡萄我会吸出果汁 [1]

我需要你，就像我的脑袋需要绞索

再见吉米·里德，再见，后会有期

我以为我可以抗拒她，但我错了


上帝与你同在，亲爱的兄弟

如果你不介意我问，是什么把你带到这里

哦，没什么，我只是在找那个人

我来看看他在这片失落的土地上躺在哪里

再见吉米·里德和你心中的一切

你听不见我在弗吉尼亚 [2] 的呼唤吗

---

[1] 参见希腊神话中酒神狄俄尼索斯的典故。

[2] 典出吉米·里德 1969 年的专辑《在弗吉尼亚》(*Down in Virginia*)。

# MOTHER OF MUSES

Mother of Muses sing for me
Sing of the mountains and the deep dark sea
Sing of the lakes and the nymphs in the forest
Sing your hearts out—all you women of the chorus
Sing of honor and fame and of glory be
Mother of Muses, sing for me

Mother of Muses sing for my heart
Sing for a love too soon to depart
Sing of the Heroes who stood alone
Whose names are engraved on tablets of stone
Who struggled with pain so the world could go free
Mother of Muses, sing for me

Sing of Sherman—Montgomery and Scott
Sing of Zhukov and Patton and the battles they fought
Who cleared the path for Presley to sing

# 缪斯之母

缪斯之母为我歌唱

歌唱高山和深沉幽暗的大海

歌唱湖泊和森林中的仙女

唱出你们的心——歌队的女子们

歌唱尊贵、盛名和荣耀

缪斯之母，为我歌唱


缪斯之母为我的心歌唱

歌唱太早离开的爱情

歌唱孑然独立的英雄

他们的名字刻在石碑

他们曾痛苦抗争让世界自由

缪斯之母，为我歌唱


歌唱谢尔曼——蒙哥马利和斯科特

歌唱朱可夫和巴顿还有他们的战斗 [1]

他们为猫王的歌声扫清了道路

---

[1] 这里所指的是美国南北战争时期的北军将领威廉·谢尔曼（William Tecumseh Sherman）和温菲尔德·斯科特（Winfield Scott），以及二战时期的盟军将领伯纳德·蒙哥马利（Bernard Montgomery）、格奥尔吉·朱可夫（Georgy Zhukov）和乔治·巴顿（George S. Patton）。

Who carved out the path for Martin Luther King
Who did what they did and then went on their way
Man, I could tell their stories all day

I'm falling in love with Calliope
She doesn't belong to anybody—why not give her to me
She's speaking to me, speaking with her eyes
I've grown so tired of chasing lies
Mother of Muses wherever you are
I've already outlived my life by far

Mother of Muses unleash your wrath
Things I can't see—they're blocking my path
Show me your wisdom—tell me my fate
Put me upright—make me walk straight
Forge my identity from the inside out
You know what I'm talking about

Take me to the river and release your charms
Let me lay down in your sweet lovin' arms
Wake me—shake me—free me from sin
Make me invisible like the wind
Got a mind to ramble—got a mind to roam
I'm travelin' light and I'm slow coming home

他们为马丁·路德·金开辟了道路
他们做了他们所做的然后继续前行
啊我可以整天讲他们的故事


我爱上了卡利俄佩 [1]
她不属于任何人——为什么不把她给我
她在跟我说话，用她的眼睛说话
我已经厌倦了追逐谎言
无论你身在何处，缪斯之母
我已远比我的一生活得更长


缪斯之母释放你的愤怒
我看不到的东西——挡住了我的去路
让我看见你的智慧——告诉我我的命运
让我站立——让我直走
从内到外塑造我的身份
你知道我在说些什么


带我去河边释放你的魅力
让我躺卧在你甜蜜的爱怀
叫醒我——撼动我——让我脱离罪恶
让我像风一样隐形
有心去漫步——有心去云游
我轻装上阵，我流连许久


---

[1] 希腊神话中宙斯之女，音乐之神，九位缪斯女神之一，被称为"荷马的缪斯"。

# CROSSING THE RUBICON

I crossed the Rubicon on the 14th day of the most dangerous
   month of the year
At the worst time at the worst place—that's all I seem to hear
I got up early so I could greet the Goddess of the Dawn
I painted my wagon—I abandoned all hope and I crossed
   the Rubicon

The Rubicon is the Red River, going gently as she flows
Redder than your ruby lips and the blood that flows from
   the rose
Three miles north of purgatory—one step from the great beyond
I prayed to the cross and I kissed the girls, and I crossed
   the Rubicon

What are these dark days I see in this world so badly bent
How can I redeem the time—the time so idly spent
How much longer can it last—how long can this go on

## 越过卢比孔河 [1]

我在一年中最危险月份的第 14 天越过了
　　卢比孔河
在最糟糕的时间在最糟糕的地方——这是我所听到的全部
我起得很早，所以我可以和黎明女神打招呼
我画下了我的马车——我弃绝了所有希望 [2]，我越过
　　卢比孔河

卢比孔河是红河，她流淌时轻轻地流淌
比你红宝石般的嘴唇和玫瑰流出的血
　　还红
炼狱以北三英里——距离伟大的彼岸一步之遥
我向十字架祈祷，我亲吻姑娘们，我越过
　　卢比孔河

我在这个弯曲的世界上看见的这些幽暗的日子是什么
我怎样才能挽回时间——浪费掉的时间
还能继续多久——这还能持续多久

---

[1] 这首歌个别句子和实际录音版本有出入。歌名典出恺撒穿越卢比孔
　　河的历史故事，意指走上了一条不归路。

[2] 参见但丁《神曲·地狱篇》第三章，第九行："进入此地的人哪，你
　　们都当弃绝指望。"（"Abandon all hope, ye who enter here."）

I embraced my love put down my head and I crossed
 the Rubicon


I can feel the bones beneath my skin and they're tremblin'
 with rage
I'll make your wife a widow—you'll never see old age
The summer meadows had turned to gold and the winter chill
 was gone
I pawned my watch and I paid my debts, and I crossed
 the Rubicon


Put my heart upon the hill where some happiness I'll find
If I survive then let me love—let the hour be mine
Take the high road—take the low, take any one you're on
I poured the cup and I passed it along and I crossed
 the Rubicon


Right or wrong? What can I say? What is it that needs
 to be said?
I'll spill your brains out on the ground—you'll be better
 off over there with the dead
Seems like ten maybe twenty years—I've been gone
I stood between heaven and earth, and I crossed the Rubicon

我拥抱了我的爱人，我低下头我，越过
　　卢比孔河


我能感觉到我皮肤下的骨头它们因愤怒
　　而颤抖
我会让你的妻子成为寡妇——你活不到老的一天 [1]
夏天的草地变成金色，冬天的寒冷
　　已消失
我当了我的表，我还了我的债，我越过
　　卢比孔河


把我的心放在山上，在那里我会找到幸福
如果我能活下来，那就让我去爱——让时间属于我
走高路——走低路，走任何你在走的路
我满上杯子，我递了过去，我越过
　　卢比孔河


对还是错？我能说什么？又有什么
　　需要说的？
我会把你的大脑洒在地上——在那儿你和死人
　　在一起会过得更好
看起来已经十年二十年了——我走之后
我站在天地之间，我越过卢比孔河

---

[1]　参见荷马《伊利亚特》第六卷。

I feel the Holy Spirit inside and see the light that freedom gives

I believe it's within the reach of every man who lives

The dyin' sun was going down and the night was comin' on

I turned the key and broke it off, and I crossed the Rubicon

Mona Baby, are you still in my mind—I truly believe that
  you are

Couldn't be anybody else but you who's come with me this far

The killing frost is on the ground and the early days are gone

I lit the torch, looked to the east and I crossed the Rubicon

我感受到心中的圣灵，看到自由所赐的光
我相信每个活着的人都触手可及
垂死的太阳正在下山，黑夜即将来临
我转动钥匙，我把它折断，我越过卢比孔河

莫娜宝贝 [1]，你还在我的心里吗——我真的
　　相信还在
不可能是其他人，除了和我一起走这么远的你
严霜覆盖大地，早先的日子已经过去
我点燃火炬，我向东望去，我越过卢比孔河

---

[1]　参见迪伦 1966 年的歌曲《再次困在莫比尔和孟菲斯蓝调一起》
（"Stuck Inside of Mobile with the Memphis Blues Again"）。

## KEY WEST
## (PHILOSOPHER PIRATE)

McKinley hollered—McKinley squalled

Doctor said McKinley—death is on the wall

Say it to me if you got something to confess

I heard all about it—he was going down slow

Heard it on the wireless radio

From down in the boondocks—way down in Key West

I'm searchin' for love and inspiration

On that pirate radio station

It's comin' out of Luxembourg and Budapest

Radio signal clear as can be

I'm so deep in love I can hardly see

Down in the flatlands—way down in Key West

Key West is the place to be

If you're lookin' for immortality

Stay on the road—follow the highway sign

# 基韦斯特 [1]
## （哲学家海盗）


麦金莱大喊——麦金莱大叫 [2]

医生说麦金莱——死亡就在眼前

如果你有什么要说的，就告诉我

我听说了——他走得很慢

在无线电台上听到的

从贫民窟那里——在基韦斯特


我在寻找爱和灵感

在那个海盗电台

它来自卢森堡和布达佩斯

无线电信号已最清晰

我爱得太深我几乎看不见

在平原上——在基韦斯特


基韦斯特是该去的地方

如果你在寻找不朽

顺着路走——按照高速公路的标志

---

[1] 基韦斯特（Key West），位于美国佛罗里达州最南部。

[2] 威廉·麦金莱（William McKinley），美国第 25 任总统，1901 年被
刺杀。

Key West is fine and fair
If you lost your mind, you'll find it there
Key West is on the horizon line

I was born on the wrong side of the railroad track
Like Ginsberg, Corso and Kerouac
Like Louie and Jimmy and Buddy and all of the rest
It might not be the thing to do
But I'm stickin' with you through and through
Down in the flatlands—way down in Key West

I got both my feet planted square on the ground
Got my right hand high with the thumb down
Such is life—such is happiness
Hibiscus flowers grow everywhere here
If you wear one put it behind your ear
Down on the bottom—way down in Key West

Key West is the place to go
Down by the Gulf of Mexico
Beyond the sea—beyond the shifting sand
Key West is the gateway key

基韦斯特一切都好

如果你失去了理智，你会在那里找回

基韦斯特在地平线上


我出生在铁轨的错误一侧

就像金斯堡、科索和凯鲁亚克 [1]

就像路易、吉米、巴迪 [2] 和其他所有人一样

这可能不是该做的事

但我一直要和你在一起

在平原上——在基韦斯特


我的双脚踩在大地上

右手高举，拇指朝下

这就是生活——这就是幸福

木槿花在这里随处可见

如果你要戴一朵花，就戴在你的耳后

在底部——在基韦斯特


基韦斯特是该去的地方

在墨西哥湾那里

在大海那边——在流沙那边

基韦斯特是进门的钥匙

--------

[1] 这 3 位是著名的美国"垮掉派"作家。

[2] 指的是 3 位美国音乐家路易斯·乔丹（Louis Jordan）、吉米·里德（Jimmy Reed）和巴迪·霍利（Buddy Holly）。

To innocence and purity
Key West—Key West is the enchanted land

I've never lived in the land of Oz
Or wasted my time with an unworthy cause
It's hot down here and you can't be overdressed
The tiny blossoms of a toxic plant
They can make you dizzy—I'd like to help ya but I can't
Down in the flatlands—way down in Key West

The fishtail ponds and the orchid trees
They can give you the bleedin' heart disease
People tell me—I oughta try a little tenderness
Amelia Street—Bay View Park
Walkin' in the shadows after dark
Down under—way down in Key West

I play the gumbo limbo spirituals
I know all the Hindu rituals
People tell me that I'm truly blessed
Bougainvillea bloomin' in the summer and spring

通往天真和纯洁

基韦斯特——基韦斯特是一片着魔的土地

我从未在奥兹国 [1] 生活

或是为了不值得的事业浪费时间

这里很热，你不能穿得太好

一种有毒植物的小花

会让你头晕目眩——我想帮助你，但我不能

在平原上——在基韦斯特

鱼尾葵池和羊蹄甲树

会让你的心流出血来

人们告诉我——我应该尝试一点温柔

阿米利亚街 [2]——湾景公园 [3]

天黑后走在阴影中

在那里——在基韦斯特

我播放那里的土著灵歌

我知道所有的印度教仪式

人们告诉我，我真的被祝福

九重葛在夏季和春季开花

---

[1] 典出莱曼·弗兰克·鲍姆（L. Frank Baum）的《绿野仙踪》（*The Wonderful Wizard of Oz*）。

[2] 基韦斯特的一条街。

[3] 基韦斯特的一个公园。

Winter here is an unknown thing
Down the flatlands—way down in Key West

Key West is under the sun
Under the radar—under the gun
You stay to the left and then you lean to the right
Feel the sunlight on your skin
And the healing virtues of the wind
Key West—Key West is the land of light

Wherever I travel—wherever I roam
I'm not that far from the convent home
I do what I think is right—what I think is best
Mystery Street off Mallory Square
Truman had his White House there
Eastbound—westbound
Way down in Key West

Twelve years old and they put me in a suit
Forced me to marry a prostitute
There were gold fringes on her wedding dress

冬天在这里是件不为人知的事

在平原上——在基韦斯特

基韦斯特在阳光下

在雷达下——在枪口下

你留在左边，然后你向右倾斜

感受阳光照在你的皮肤上

还有风的疗愈功效

基韦斯特——基韦斯特是光明之地

无论我在哪里旅行——无论我在哪里漫游

我都离那修道院不远

我做我认为正确的事——我认为最好的事

马洛里广场 [1] 附近的神秘街 [2]

杜鲁门在那里有他的白宫

往东走——往西走

在基韦斯特

十二岁他们让我穿上西装

逼我和一个妓女结婚

她的婚纱上有金色的流苏

---

[1]　马洛里广场，也叫日落广场，基韦斯特的一个广场。

[2]　参考《神秘街》（"Mystery Street"），J. 霍华德（J. Howard）、J. 普兰特（J. Plante）、P. 杰拉德（P. Gerard）和 J. 格里森（J. Gleason）等 1953 年的歌曲。

That's my story but not where it ends
She's still cute and we're still friends
Down in the bottom—way down in Key West

I play both sides against the middle
Pickin' up that pirate radio signal
I heard the news—I heard your last request
Fly around my Pretty Little Miss
I don't love nobody—gimme a kiss
Down at the bottom—way down in Key West

Key West is the place to be
If you're lookin' for immortality
Key West is paradise divine
Key West is fine and fair
If you lost your mind you'll find it there
Key West is on the horizon line

这是我的故事，但不是结束

她依然很美，我们依然是朋友

在底部——在基韦斯特

我代表两边攻击中间

接收海盗无线电信号

我听到了新闻——我听到了你最后的请求

绕着我的漂亮小姐飞翔 [1]

我不爱任何人——给我一个吻

在底部——在基韦斯特

基韦斯特是该去的地方

如果你在寻找不朽

基韦斯特是神圣的乐园

基韦斯特一切都好

如果你失去了理智，你会在那里找回

基韦斯特在地平线上

---

[1] 《绕着我的漂亮小姐飞翔》（"Fly around My Pretty Little Miss"）是一
首美国民谣歌曲。

# MURDER MOST FOUL

'Twas a dark day in Dallas—November '63

The day that will live on in infamy

President Kennedy was riding high

A good day to be living and a good day to die

Being led to the slaughter like a sacrificial lamb

Say wait a minute boys, do you know who I am?

Of course we do, we know who you are

Then they blew off his head when he was still in the car

Shot down like a dog in broad daylight

'Twas a matter of timing and the timing was right

You got unpaid debts and we've come to collect

We're gon' kill you with hatred and without any respect

We'll mock you and shock you, we'll grin in your face

We've already got someone here to take your place

The day that they blew out the brains of the king

Thousands were watching, no one saw a thing

It happened so quickly—so quick by surprise

Right there in front of everyone's eyes


Greatest magic trick ever under the sun

## 最卑鄙的谋杀 *[1]

这是达拉斯 [2] 黑暗的一天——1963 年 11 月

这一天将会恶名昭彰

肯尼迪总统那时意气风发

这是一个活着的好日子，这是一个去死的好日子

像献祭的羔羊一样被带去宰杀

说等一下小伙子们，你们知道我是谁吗？

我们当然知道，我们知道你是谁

然后他们爆了他的头，当他还在车里时

在光天化日之下像狗一样被打死

这是一个时机问题，时机正好

你有未还的债，我们来收

我们会杀死你，带着仇恨，毫无尊敬

我们会嘲笑你，让你震惊，我们会当着你的面大笑

我们已经找到人来接替你了

他们炸掉国王大脑的那一天

成千上万的人在看，没有人看清什么

发生得如此之快——出乎意料地如此之快

就在每个人的眼前


日光之下最伟大的魔术

\* 本诗注释数量较多，故采取文后注的形式。——编者注

Perfectly executed, skillfully done

Wolfman, oh wolfman, oh wolfman, howl

Rub a dub dub—it's murder most foul


Hush lil children, you'll soon understand

The Beatles are coming they're gonna hold your hand

Slide down the banister, go get your coat

Ferry 'cross the Mersey and go for the throat

There's three bums comin' all dressed in rags

Pick up the pieces and lower the flags

I'm going to Woodstock, it's the Aquarian Age

Then I'll go over to Altamont and sit near the stage

Put your head out the window, let the good times roll

There's a party going on behind the grassy knoll

Stack up the bricks and pour the cement

Don't say Dallas don't love you, Mr. President

Put your foot in the tank and step on the gas

Try to make it to the triple underpass

Black face singer—white face clown

Better not show your faces after the sun goes down


I'm in the red-light district like a cop on the beat

Living in a nightmare on Elm Street

When you're down on Deep Ellum put your money
    in your shoe

Don't ask what your country can do for you

完美执行，巧妙完成

狼人 [3]，哦狼人，哦狼人，嚎叫吧 [4]

啦哒哒哒 [5]——这是最卑鄙的谋杀


嘘，孩子们 [6]，你们很快就会明白的

披头士要来了，他们会牵着你的手 [7]

滑下扶手，去拿你的外套

渡轮穿过默西河 [8]，直奔咽喉 [9]

三个流浪汉来了，都穿着破烂衣服 [10]

收拾残局，降下旗帜

我要去伍德斯托克 [11]，这是水瓶座时代 [12]

然后我会去阿尔塔蒙特 [13] 坐在舞台附近

把头伸出窗外，让美好时光滚滚而来 [14]

草丘 [15] 后面正举行派对 [16]

把砖堆起来，倒上水泥

不要说达拉斯不爱你，总统先生 [17]

伸出脚使劲踩下油门

尝试进入三重地下通道

黑脸歌手 [18]——白脸小丑

太阳下山后最好不要露面


我在红灯区像个巡逻的警察

住在艾姆街的噩梦中 [19]

当你走在迪普艾鲁姆把钱放在

　　你的鞋子里 [20]

不要问你的国家能为你做什么 [21]

Cash on the barrel head, money to burn

Dealey Plaza, make a left hand turn

Go down to the crossroads, try to flag a ride

That's the place where Faith, Hope and Charity died

Shoot 'em while he runs, boy, shoot 'em while you can

See if you can shoot the Invisible Man

Goodbye, Charlie, goodbye Uncle Sam

Frankly, Miss Scarlet, I don't give a damn

What is the truth and where did it go

Ask Oswald and Ruby—they oughta know

Shut your mouth, says the wise old owl

Business is business and it's murder most foul

Tommy can you hear me, I'm the Acid Queen

I'm ridin' in a long black Lincoln limousine

Ridin' in the back seat, next to my wife

Heading straight on into the afterlife

I'm leaning to the left, got my head in her lap

Oh Lord, I've been led into some kind of a trap

We ask no quarter, no quarter do we give

We're right down the street from the street where you live

They mutilated his body and took out his brain

What more could they do, they piled on the pain

But his soul was not there where it was supposed to be at

For the last fifty years they've been searching for that

Freedom, oh freedom, freedom over me

全都靠钞票，花不完的钱 [22]

迪利广场 [23]，在那里左转

走到十字路口 [24]，尝试搭个便车

那是信、望、爱死掉的地方

趁他跑的时候对他们射击，小伙子，尽可能对他们射击 [25]

看看你能不能射杀隐形人 [26]

再见，查理 [27]，再见山姆大叔 [28]

说实话，斯嘉丽小姐 [29]，我不在乎

真相是什么，它去了哪里

问奥斯瓦尔德 [30] 和鲁比 [31]——他们应该知道

闭上你的嘴，聪明的老猫头鹰 [32] 说

生意就是生意 [33]，这是最卑鄙的谋杀


汤米你能听到我吗，我是迷幻药女王 [34]

我乘坐一辆黑色长款林肯轿车 [35]

坐在后座 [36]，在我妻子旁边

直奔死后的世界

我向左倒下，头落在她的腿上

哦主啊，我被带进了某种陷阱

我们不要求怜悯 [37]，我们也不会怜悯

我们就在你居住的街对面 [38]

他们肢解了他的身体，他们取出了他的大脑 [39]

他们还能做什么，他们又堆积了痛苦

但他的灵魂并不在该在的地方

过去的五十年里，他们一直在寻找

自由，哦自由，自由比我重要 [40]

Hate to tell you, Mister, but only dead men are free

Send me some loving—tell me no lie

Throw the gun in the gutter and walk on by

Wake up, Little Suzie, let's go for a drive

Cross the Trinity River, let's keep hope alive

Turn the radio on, don't touch the dials

Parkland Hospital's only six more miles

You got me dizzy Miss Lizzy, you filled me with lead

That magic bullet of yours has gone to my head

I'm just a patsy like Patsy Cline

I never shot anyone from in front or behind

Got blood in my eyes, got blood in my ear

I'm never gonna make it to the New Frontier

Zapruder's film, I've seen that before

Seen it thirty three times, maybe more

It's vile and deceitful—it's cruel and it's mean

Ugliest thing that you ever have seen

They killed him once, they killed him twice

Killed him like a human sacrifice

The day that they killed him, someone said to me, "Son,

The age of the anti-Christ has just only begun."

Air Force One coming in through the gate

Johnson sworn in at two thirty-eight

Let me know when you decide to throw in the towel

It is what it is and it's murder most foul

本不想告诉你，先生，但只有死人是自由的
给我一些爱 [41]——不要对我说谎
把枪扔进水沟然后若无其事地走开 [42]
醒来，小苏西 [43]，我们去兜风
跨过三一河 [44]，让我们保持希望
打开收音机，不要碰旋钮
帕克兰医院 [45] 还有六英里
你让我头晕丽兹小姐 [46]，你给我灌了铅
你的那颗灵丹妙药进了我的脑子 [47]
我只是像佩茜·克莱恩 [48] 一样的替罪羊
我从不从前面或后面射杀任何人
我的眼睛里有血，我的耳朵里有血
我永远到不了新边疆 [49]


泽普鲁德 [50] 的电影，我以前看过
看过三十三遍，也许更多
是卑鄙而虚假的——是残酷的，是刻薄的
是你见过的最丑的
他们杀了他一次，他们杀了他两次
像人祭一样把他杀死
他们杀死他的那天，有人对我说："孩子，
敌基督者的时代才刚刚开始。"
空军一号从大门进来
约翰逊 [51] 两点三十八分宣誓就职
当你决定认输时告诉我
事情就是这样，这是最卑鄙的谋杀

What's New Pussycat—what'd I say
I said the soul of a nation been torn away
It's beginning to go down into a slow decay
And that it's thirty-six hours past judgment day
Wolfman Jack, he's speaking in tongues
He's going on and on at the top of his lungs
Play me a song, Mr. Wolfman Jack
Play it for me in my long Cadillac
Play that Only The Good Die Young
Take me to the place where Tom Dooley was hung
Play St. James Infirmary in the court of King James
If you want to remember, better write down the names
Play Etta James too, play I'd Rather Go Blind
Play it for the man with the telepathic mind
Play John Lee Hooker play Scratch My Back
Play it for that strip club owner named Jack
Guitar Slim—Goin' Down Slow
Play it for me and for Marilyn Monroe
And please, Don't Let Me Be Misunderstood
Play it for the First Lady, she ain't feeling that good
Play Don Henley—play Glenn Frey
Take it to the Limit and let it go by
And play it for Carl Wilson, too
Lookin' far, far away down Gower Avenue
Play Tragedy, play Twilight Time

《小妞最近怎么了》[52]——我怎么说[53]

我说一个国家的灵魂被撕裂了

从此开始慢慢腐烂

审判日过后三十六小时

狼人杰克，他在说方言

他在声嘶力竭地继续讲

给我放一首歌，狼人杰克先生

在我长长的凯迪拉克中为我播放

播放《只有好人死得年轻》[54]

带我去汤姆·杜利[55]被绞死的地方

在詹姆斯国王的王宫里播放《圣詹姆斯医院》[56]

如果想要记住，最好写下名字

还要放埃塔·詹姆丝[57]，放《我宁愿看不见》[58]

给有心灵感应的那个人播放

播放约翰·李·胡克[59]播放《宝贝，帮帮我》[60]

为那个名叫杰克的脱衣舞俱乐部老板[61]播放

吉他斯利姆[62]—《慢慢来》[63]

为我播放，为玛丽莲·梦露播放

请为我们播放《请不要让我被误解》[64]

为第一夫人播放，她感觉不太舒服

播放唐·亨利——播放格伦·弗雷[65]

《推向极限》[66]，让它过去

也为卡尔·威尔逊[67]播放

远远地看着高尔大道[68]

播放《悲剧》[69]，播放《黄昏时分》[70]

Take Me Back to Tulsa to the scene of the crime

Play another one and Another One Bites the Dust

Play the Old Rugged Cross and in G-d We Trust

Ride the Pink Horse down that Long, Lonesome Road

Stand there and wait for his head to explode

Play Mystery Train for Mr. Mystery

The man who fell down dead, like a rootless tree

Play it for the Reverend, play it for the Pastor

Play it for the dog that's got no master

Play Oscar Peterson and play Stan Getz

Play Blue Sky, play Dickie Betts


Play Art Pepper, play Thelonious Monk

Charlie Parker and all that junk

All that junk and All That Jazz

Play something for The Birdman of Alcatraz

Play Buster Keaton play Harold Lloyd

Play Bugsy Siegel play Pretty Boy Floyd

Play all the numbers, play all the odds

Play Cry Me A River for the Lord of the Gods

Play number nine, play number six

Play it for Lindsey and Stevie Nicks

Play Nat King Cole, play Nature Boy

Play Down in the Boondocks for Terry Malloy

Play It Happened One Night and One Night of Sin

There's twelve million souls that are listening in

带我回到塔尔萨到犯罪现场 [71]

再放一个，《又倒下一个》[72]

放《古旧十架》和《我们信靠上帝》[73]

骑着粉红马沿着那漫长而寂寞的路走 [74]

站在那里等他的脑袋爆炸

为神秘先生 [75] 放《神秘列车》[76]

倒地死去的人像一棵无根的树

为牧师播放 [77]，为传道人播放

为没有主人的狗播放

播放奥斯卡·彼得森 [78]，播放斯坦·盖茨 [79]

放《蓝天》[80]，放迪基·贝茨 [81]


放阿特·佩珀 [82]，放塞隆尼斯·蒙克 [83]

查理·帕克 [84] 和所有的瘾君子

所有的瘾君子和所有的爵士乐 [85]

为恶魔岛的鸟人 [86] 放点东西

放巴斯特·基顿 [87] 放哈罗德·劳埃德 [88]

放小虫西格尔放漂亮男孩弗洛伊德 [89]

押注所有数字，赌上所有可能

为众神之主播放《泪流成河》[90]

放九号，放六号 [91]

为林赛·白金汉 [92] 和史蒂薇·尼克斯 [93] 播放

放纳京高 [94]，放《纯真男孩》[95]

为特里·马洛伊 [96] 放《在穷乡僻壤》[97]

播放《一夜风流》[98] 和《一夜的罪》[99]

有一千二百万个灵魂在聆听

Play the Merchant of Venice, play the merchants of death

Play Stella by Starlight for Lady Macbeth

Don't worry Mr. President, help's on the way

Your brothers are comin', there'll be hell to pay

Brothers? What brothers? What's this about hell?

Tell 'em we're waitin'—keep coming—we'll get 'em as well

Love Field is where his plane touched down

But it never did get back up off of the ground

Was a hard act to follow, second to none

They killed him on the Altar of the Rising Sun

Play Misty for me and that Old Devil Moon

Play Anything Goes and Memphis in June

Play Lonely at the Top and Lonely Are the Brave

Play it for Houdini spinning around in his grave

Play Jelly Roll Morton, play Lucille

Play Deep in a Dream and play Drivin' Wheel

Play Moonlight Sonata in F sharp

And Key to the Highway by the king of the harp

Play Marchin' Through Georgia and Dumbarton's Drums

Play Darkness and death will come when it comes

Play Love Me or Leave Me by the great Bud Powell

Play the Blood Stained Banner—play Murder Most Foul

放《威尼斯商人》，放死亡商人 [100]

为麦克白夫人播放《星光下的史黛拉》[101]

总统先生别担心，救援正在路上

你的兄弟们来了 [102]，要付出地狱一般的代价

兄弟们？什么兄弟们？这跟地狱有什么关系？

告诉他们我们在等着——快来——我们也会杀了他们

"爱场" [103] 是他的飞机降落的地方

但飞机再也没有离开地面

难以模仿的行为，绝对首屈一指

他们在日升祭坛 [104] 上杀死了他

为我播放《雾蒙蒙》[105] 和《老恶魔月亮》[106]

放《海上情缘》[107] 和《六月的孟菲斯》[108]

播放《高高在上的孤独》[109]，还有《自古英雄多寂寞》[110]

为坟墓里转着圈的胡迪尼 [111] 播放

放杰利·罗尔·莫顿 [112]，放露西尔 [113]

放《深入梦乡》[114] 并放《驱动轮》[115]

放《升 F 大调月光奏鸣曲》[116]

和口琴之王的《公路钥匙》[117]

放《进军佐治亚》[118] 和《邓巴顿的鼓》[119]

播放《黑暗》[120]，死亡该来就会来

播放伟大的巴德·鲍威尔的《爱我或离开我》[121]

播放《血染旗帜》[122]——播放最卑鄙的谋杀

[1] 典出莎士比亚《哈姆雷特》第一幕第五场："杀人是重大的罪恶；可是这一件谋杀的惨案，更是骇人听闻而逆天害理的罪行。"（"Murder most foul, as in the best it is / But this most foul, strange and unnatural."）

[2] 达拉斯（Dallas）是美国得克萨斯州第三大城市。

[3] 沃夫曼·杰克（Wolfman Jack，真名 Robert Weston Smith），即"狼人杰克"，美国著名音乐节目主持人。

[4] 《狼人嚎叫》（"Wolfman Howl"）是"颤音器"乐队（The Vibrators）1982 年的歌曲。

[5] 典出童谣《啦哒哒哒》（"Rub-A-Dub-Dub"）。

[6] 典出童谣《睡吧，小宝贝》（"Hush Little Baby"）。

[7] 《我想牵着你的手》（"I Want to Hold Your Hand"）是"披头士"乐队（The Beatles）的歌曲。

[8] 默西河（River Mersey）是英格兰西北部的河流。

[9] 典出"加里和领跑者"乐队的歌曲《渡轮穿过默西河》（"Ferry Cross the Mersey"）。

[10] 指达拉斯地区的几位摄影记者拍摄到的 3 流浪汉，他们也成了阴谋论者讨论的主题，被认为可能参与了刺杀行动。

[11] 指 1969 年 8 月 15 到 18 日举办的伍德斯托克音乐节，吸引了超过 40 万参加者。

[12] 伍德斯托克音乐节被宣传为"水瓶座博览会：3 天的和平与音乐"。

[13] 指阿尔塔蒙特自由音乐会，1969 年 12 月 6 日星期六在美国举行的一场摇滚音乐会。

[14] 典出《让美好时光滚滚而来》（"Let the Good Times Roll"），感恩而死乐队（Grateful Dead）、比·比·金（B. B. King）、路易斯·乔丹（Louis Jordan）、音乐二人组 Shirley & Lee 等都唱过同名歌曲。

[15] 阴谋论暗示，杀害约翰·菲茨杰拉德·肯尼迪（John Fitzgerald Kennedy）的真正的刺客是一位身份不明的枪手，潜伏在一个长满草的小山丘上。

[16] 参考万达·杰克逊（Wanda Jackson）的歌曲《一场派对正进行》（"There's a Party Goin' On"）。

[17]　1963 年 11 月 22 日，娜莉·康纳利（Nellie Connally）和她的丈夫、得克萨斯州州长约翰·康纳利以及肯尼迪一起乘坐豪华轿车。康纳利对肯尼迪总统说："总统先生，你不能说达拉斯不爱你。"（"Mr. President, you can't say Dallas doesn't love you."）肯尼迪总统承认说："不，你当然不能。"（"No, you certainly can't."）几秒钟后，她听到了刺杀总统的枪响。

[18]　白人把脸涂黑扮演黑人是美国曾经的戏剧传统，有种族歧视嫌疑。

[19]　典出美国导演韦斯·克雷文（Wes Craven）1984 年的电影《猛鬼街》（*A Nightmare on Elm Street*）。也暗指肯尼迪遇刺时的街名。

[20]　典出《迪普艾鲁姆布鲁斯》（"Deep Elm Blues"，有时也写作"Deep Elem Blues"或"Deep Ellum Blues"），感恩而死乐队的歌曲。迪普艾鲁姆（Deep Ellum）是达拉斯娱乐区，也称 Deep Elm 或者 Deep Elem，或与上文艾姆街（Elm Street）相呼应。

[21]　典出肯尼迪总统的就职演说。

[22]　典出两首美国乡村歌曲音乐组合"深情兄弟"（The Louvin Brothers）的《全都靠钞票》（"Cash on the Barrelhead"）和乔治·琼斯（George Jones）的《花不完的钱》（"Money to Burn"）。

[23]　迪利广场（Dealey Plaza）是位于美国得克萨斯州达拉斯市中心街区西区（West End）的一个小广场，1963 年 11 月 22 日美国总统约翰·肯尼迪在这里遭到枪击身亡。

[24]　参见美国布鲁斯音乐家、歌曲创作者罗伯特·约翰逊（Robert Johnson）的歌曲《十字路口》（"Cross Road Blues"）。

[25]　典出 20 世纪 60 年代美国多种乐器演奏家朱尼尔·沃克（Junior Walker）的乐队"朱尼尔·沃克与群星"（Jr. Walker & The All Stars）的歌曲《猎枪》（"Shotgun"）。

[26]　典出拉尔夫·艾里森的《看不见的人》（*Invisible Man*）。英文中射杀（shoot）和摄影是同一个词。

[27]　典出美国舞台指导、导演文森特·明奈利（Vincente Minnelli）1964 年导演的电影《再见，查理！》（*Goodbye, Charlie*）。另外，越战时美国通常称越南共产党为越共（Viet Cong），简称 VC，在军事字母代码中被称为"维克多·查理"（Victor Charlie），因此"查理"也指代越共。

[28]　"山姆大叔"（Uncle Sam）常指代美国。

[29]　斯嘉丽小姐（Miss Scarlett），玛格丽特·米切尔（Margaret Munnerlyn Mitchell）1936 年的小说《飘》（*Gone with the Wind*）女主人

127

公。小说后被改编为著名电影《乱世佳人》。这句话暗合了电影的台词。

[30] 李·哈维·奥斯瓦尔德（Lee Harvey Oswald），1963 年 11 月 22 日暗杀美国第 35 任总统约翰·F. 肯尼迪的凶手。

[31] 杰克·鲁比（Jack Leon Ruby），一家美国夜总会的老板，据称是芝加哥黑帮的同伙，于 1963 年 11 月 24 日，奥斯瓦尔德被指控暗杀约翰·F. 肯尼迪总统两天之后，谋杀了奥斯瓦尔德。

[32] 典出美国 20 世纪三四十年代乐队领队、广播名人凯·科瑟（Kay Kyser）的歌曲《聪明的老猫头鹰》（"The Wise Old Owl"）。

[33] 此处为一英语习惯用法。

[34] 参考英国摇滚乐队"谁人"（The Who）1969 年专辑《汤米》（*Tommy*）的两首歌《汤米你能听到我吗》（"Tommy Can You Hear Me?"）和《迷幻药女王》（"The Acid Queen"）。

[35] 参考"猫王"埃尔维斯·普雷斯利（Elvis Presley）的《黑色长款豪华轿车》（"Long Black Limousine"）。

[36] 典出美国乐队"满室布鲁斯"（Roomful of Blues）的《后座布鲁斯》（"Backseat Blues"）。

[37] 参考"齐柏林飞艇"乐队（Led Zeppelin）1973 年的歌曲《无情无义》（"No Quarter"）。

[38] 典出约翰·迈克尔·金（John Michael King）的《你居住的街道》（"On the Street Where You Live"）。

[39] 华盛顿国家档案馆中肯尼迪的大脑 1964 年后神秘失踪。

[40] 参考美国民谣歌手琼·贝兹（Joan Baez）的民权歌曲《哦，自由》（"Oh Freedom"）。

[41] 典出美国音乐家、歌手、歌曲创作者小理查德（Little Richard）的《给我一些爱》（"Send Me Some Lovin'"）。

[42] 典出美国音乐家伯特·巴卡拉克（Burt Bacharach）的《若无其事地走开》（"Walk On By"）。

[43] 典出美国音乐组合艾佛利兄弟（The Everly Brothers）1957 年的歌曲《小苏西》（"Wake Up Little Susie"）。

[44] 三一河（Trinity River），美国得克萨斯州境内最长的有分水岭的河流。

[45] 帕克兰医院，肯尼迪遇刺后被送往的医院。

[46] 典出《你让我头晕，丽兹小姐》（"Dizzy, Miss Lizzy"）。此曲最早是 1958 年拉里·威廉姆斯（Larry Williams）的摇滚经典歌曲，后

被"披头士"乐队在 1965 年的专辑《救命！》(*Help!*) 中录制并推广。

[47]  参考美国爵士乐歌手比莉·哈乐黛（Billie Holiday）的歌曲《你让我神魂颠倒》（"You Go to My Head"）。这里的"灵丹妙药"亦可理解为"子弹"。

[48]  佩茜·克莱恩（Patsy Cline）是一名美国歌手。她是 20 世纪最有影响力的歌手之一，也是最早跨入流行音乐领域的乡村音乐家之一。

[49]  "新边疆"是美国总统肯尼迪的重要政治口号。同时，美国民谣音乐组合金斯顿三重唱（The Kingston Trio）亦有歌曲《新边疆》（"The New Frontier"）。

[50]  亚伯拉罕·泽普鲁德（Abraham Zapruder），美国服装制造商。他意外地在家庭录像中捕捉到了刺杀肯尼迪的枪击事件。《泽普鲁德的电影》（*Zapruder film*）是一部无声电影，记录了 1963 年 11 月 22 日约翰·肯尼迪总统遇刺的事件。这部电影被认为是"历史上最重要的 26 秒电影"。

[51]  指林登·约翰逊（Lyndon Baines Johnson），1963 年到 1969 年担任美国第 36 任总统。他曾在 1961 年至 1963 年担任约翰·F. 肯尼迪总统的副总统，并在肯尼迪遇刺后不久宣誓就职。

[52]  典出威尔士歌手汤姆·琼斯（Tom Jones）的歌曲《小妞最近怎么了》（"What's New Pussycat?"）。

[53]  参考美国歌手雷·查尔斯（Ray Charles）1959 年的歌曲《我会说什么》（"What'd I Say"）。

[54]  《只有好人死得年轻》（"Only the Good Die Young"）是比利·乔（Billy Joel）1977 年的歌曲。

[55]  典出金斯顿三重唱（The Kingston Trio）的歌曲《汤姆·杜利》（"Tom Dooley"）。

[56]  《圣詹姆斯医院》（"St. James Infimary"）是路易斯·阿姆斯特朗（Louis Armstrong）1928 年的歌曲。

[57]  埃塔·詹姆丝（Etta James），美国布鲁斯、爵士、福音及灵歌歌手。

[58]  《我宁愿看不见》（I'd Rather Go Blind）是埃塔·詹姆丝（Etta James）1967 年的歌曲。

[59]  约翰·李·胡克（John Lee Hooker），美国布鲁斯歌手、歌曲创作者、吉他演奏者。

[60]  《宝贝，帮帮我》（"Baby Scratch My Back"）是美国布鲁斯音乐家斯利姆·哈珀（Slim Harpo）的歌曲。

[61] 杰克·鲁比（Jack Leon Ruby），就是前述打死肯尼迪暗杀者奥斯瓦尔德的人。

[62] 埃迪·琼斯（Eddie Jones），昵称"吉他斯利姆"（"Guitar Slim"）是活跃于20世纪40年代和50年代的美国吉他手，最出名的是为专业唱片公司发行的畅销歌曲《我曾经做过的事情》（"The Things That I Used to Do"）。

[63] 《慢慢来》（"Goin' Down Slow"）是埃迪·琼斯的歌曲。

[64] 《请不要让我被误解》（"Don't Let Me Be Misunderstood"）是一首经典爵士歌曲，由爵士乐传奇人物妮娜·西蒙（Nina Simone）录制，随后成为摇滚乐队动物乐团（The Animals）的热门单曲。

[65] 唐·亨利（Don Henley）和格伦·弗雷（Glenn Frey），老鹰乐队（Eagles）的成员。

[66] 《推向极限》（"Take It to the Limit"）是老鹰乐队1975年的歌曲。

[67] 卡尔·威尔逊（Carl Wilson），海滩男孩乐队（The Beach Boys)的主唱。

[68] 典出沃伦·泽文（Warren Zevon）1976年的单曲《屋檐下的亡命之徒》（"Desperados Under the Eaves"）。这首歌曲的背景人声就是卡尔·威尔逊。

[69] 《悲剧》（"Tragedy"）是弗利特伍德（The Fleetwoods）乐团的歌曲。

[70] 《黄昏时分》（"Twilight Time"）是音乐组合派特斯乐队（The Platters）1958年的歌曲。

[71] 典出《带我回到塔尔萨》（"Take Me Back to Tulsa"），西部摇摆乐队"鲍勃·威尔斯和他的得克萨斯花花公子"（Bob Wills and His Texas Playboys）的标志性歌曲之一。塔尔萨，美国地名。塔尔萨1921年发生过最严重的种族暴力事件之一。

[72] 《又倒下一个》（"Another One Bites the Dust"）是皇后乐队（Queen）1980年的歌曲。

[73] 《古旧十架》（"The Old Rugged Cross"）和《我们信靠上帝》（"In God We Trust"）均为基督教传统赞美诗。

[74] 参见盖瑟·卡尔顿（Gaither Carlton）的歌曲《沿着那条寂寞的路眺望》（"Look Down That Lonesome Road"）。另参见琼·贝兹（Joan Baez）的歌曲《寂寞的路》（"Lonesome Road"）。

[75] 参考《神秘，拉先生》（"Mystery, Mr. Ra"），美国爵士音乐家、诗人桑·拉（Sun Ra）的歌曲。

[76] 《神秘列车》（"Mystery Train"）是小帕尔克（Junior Parker）的美国

布鲁斯歌曲，后来被"猫王"翻唱。

[77]  有可能让人联想到马丁·路德·金牧师（The Reverend Martin Luther King, Jr.），美国牧师、社会活动家、黑人民权运动领袖。

[78]  奥斯卡·彼得森（Oscar Emmanuel Peterson），加拿大爵士钢琴家和作曲家。

[79]  斯坦·盖茨（Stan Getz），美国爵士萨克斯演奏家。

[80]  《蓝天》（"Blue Sky"）是奥尔曼兄弟乐队（Allman Brothers Band）的歌曲，来自他们 1972 年的专辑《吃个桃子》（*Eat a Peach*）。这首歌是由迪基·贝茨（Dickey Betts）创作和演唱的。

[81]  迪基·贝茨（Dickey Betts），美国吉他手、歌手、词曲作者和作曲家。

[82]  阿特·佩珀（Arthur Edward Pepper, Jr.），美国萨克斯演奏家。

[83]  塞隆尼斯·蒙克（Thelonious Monk），美国爵士钢琴家和作曲家。

[84]  查理·帕克（Charles Parker），昵称"大鸟"，美国爵士音乐家。

[85]  参考 1979 美国歌舞电影《爵士春秋》（*All That Jazz*）。也参考百老汇剧团音乐剧《芝加哥》中的爵士乐《爵士春秋》（"All That Jazz"）。

[86]  全名为罗伯特·富兰克林·斯特劳德（Robert Franklin Stroud），一个在监狱中饲养和出售小鸟的美国囚犯，后成为鸟类专家。他的传奇经历在 1962 年被改编成电影《恶魔岛的鸟人》（*Birdman of Alcatraz*）。

[87]  巴斯特·基顿（Buster Keaton），美国喜剧演员，美国默片时代的代表人物之一。

[88]  哈罗德·劳埃德（Harold Lloyd）与查理·卓别林（Charles Chaplin, Jr.）和巴斯特·基顿齐名为默片时代最有影响力的 3 位电影喜剧演员。

[89]  20 世纪初期，本杰明·"小虫"·西格尔（Benjamin "Bugsy" Siegel）和查尔斯·"漂亮男孩"·弗洛伊德（Charles "Pretty Boy" Floyd）都是美国犯罪界最为声名狼藉的人物。本杰明·"小虫"·西格尔又称"狂人"西格尔，是美国黑帮老大，他在拉斯维加斯建立火烈鸟酒店和赌场，最后遇刺身亡。1991 年的电影《豪情四海》（*Bugsy*）便以他的生平展开。"漂亮男孩"·弗洛伊德是美国 20 世纪 30 年代有名的银行劫匪。迪伦的民谣偶像伍迪·格思里（Woody Guthrie）也曾创作歌曲《漂亮男孩弗洛伊德》（"Pretty Boy Floyd"）。

[90]  《泪流成河》（"Cry Me a River"）是美国爵士歌手、"爵士女王"艾

拉·费兹杰拉（Ella Fitzgerald）的歌曲。

[91] 指披头士乐队的白色专辑中的《九号革命》（"Revolution 9"），而该专辑的第六首歌是《持续的故事》（"The Continuing Story of Bungalow Bill"）。

[92] 林赛·白金汉（Lindsey Buckingham），美国音乐家、歌手。

[93] 史蒂薇·尼克斯（Stevie Nicks），美国创作歌手。

[94] 纳京高（Nat King Cole），美国音乐史上的著名歌手。

[95] 《纯真男孩》（"Nature Boy"）是纳京高 1948 年发行的歌曲。

[96] 特里·马洛伊（Terry Malloy）是码头工人的名字，由马龙·白兰度（Marlon Brando）在 1954 年的电影《码头风云》（On the Waterfront）中所饰演。马洛伊最终揭露了码头工人联盟的领导人是腐败的暴徒。

[97] 《在穷乡僻壤》（"Down in the Boondocks"）是比利·乔·罗伊尔（Billy Joe Royal）1965 年的歌曲。

[98] 《一夜风流》（It Happened One Night）是克拉克·盖博（Clark Gable）和克劳黛·考尔白（Claudette Colbert）主演的电影。

[99] "猫王"埃尔维斯·普雷斯利（Elvis Presley）的歌曲《一夜的罪》（"One Night of Sin"）。

[100] 《威尼斯商人》（Merchant of Venice）是莎士比亚的一部戏剧，《死亡商人》（Merchants of Death）是一部关于世界军火贸易的书。两者都有同名电影。另外，为一战提供资金和物资的产业和银行被称为"死亡商人"（"Merchants of Death"）。

[101] 《星光下的史黛拉》（"Stella by Starlight"）是配乐大师维克多·杨（Victor Young）为 1944 年的电影《不速之客》（The Uninvited）写的一首爵士歌曲，由迈尔斯·戴维斯（Miles Davis）演唱。

[102] 约翰·F.肯尼迪的弟弟罗伯特·肯尼迪后来竞选总统时也被刺杀。

[103] 达拉斯主要机场。

[104] 典出美国民谣歌曲《日升之屋》（"House of the Rising Sun"）。

[105] 指埃罗尔·加纳（Erroll Garner）1954 年的爵士乐标准曲《雾蒙蒙》（"Misty"）和 1971 惊悚电影《迷雾追魂》（Play Misty for Me）。

[106] 《老恶魔月亮》（"Old Devil Moon"）是伯顿·莱恩（Burton Lane）在 1947 年创作，迈尔斯·戴维斯五重奏（Miles Davis Quintet）演奏的歌曲。

[107] 《海上情缘》（Anything Goes）是科尔·波特（Cole Porter）1934 年创作的歌舞剧。

[108]　《六月的孟菲斯》（"Memphis in June"）最著名的版本是妮娜·西蒙（Nina Simone）的版本。

[109]　《高高在上的孤独》（"Lonely at the Top"）最初是兰迪·纽曼（Randy Newman）写给弗兰克·辛纳特拉（Frank Sinatra）的一首歌。

[110]　《自古英雄多寂寞》（*Lonely Are the Brave*）是 1962 年的电影，根据爱德华·艾比（Edward Abbey）的小说《勇敢的牛仔》（*The Brave Cowboy*）改编而来。据称，肯尼迪于 1962 年在白宫观看了这部电影。

[111]　哈利·胡迪尼（Harry Houdini），被称为史上最伟大的魔术师，脱逃术及特技表演者。

[112]　杰利·罗尔·莫顿（Jelly Roll Morton），美国作曲家。他 1915 年的作品《杰利·罗尔布鲁斯》（*Jelly Roll Blues*）是第一部出版的爵士乐作品。此外他也是电影《海上钢琴师》（又译《1900 传奇》）中和主人公 1900 斗琴的那位大师的原型。

[113]　《露西尔》（"Lucille"）是小理查德（Little Richard）的歌曲。

[114]　《深入梦乡》（"Deep in a Dream"）是美国爵士小号手、歌手查特·贝克（Chet Baker）的歌曲。

[115]　《驱动轮》（"Driving Wheel"）是艾尔·格林（Al Green）1960 年的歌曲。

[116]　这里迪伦把升 C 小调的《月光奏鸣曲》写成 F 大调。迪伦认为贝多芬的第 24 号钢琴奏鸣曲——那首高度抒情，中等难度，不寻常的《升 F 大调奏鸣曲》比《月光奏鸣曲》更好。

[117]　《公路钥匙》（"Key to the Highway"）是美国布鲁斯音乐家（"口琴之王"）小沃尔特（Little Walter）的歌曲。美国南方有时将口琴称为 "harp"。

[118]　《进军佐治亚》（"Marching Through Georgia"），田纳西·厄尼·福特（Tennessee Ernie Ford）1865 年内战结束时的一首歌。

[119]　苏格兰民谣歌曲《邓巴顿的鼓》（"Dumbarton's Drums"）。

[120]　参考伦纳德·科恩（Leonard Norman Cohen）的歌曲《黑暗》（"Darkness"）。

[121]　巴德·鲍威尔（Bud Powell），爵士钢琴家，作曲家。这里迪伦或许记错了，巴德·鲍威尔并没有写过《爱我或离开我》。

[122]　《血染旗帜》（"The Blood-Stained Banner"）有两重含义，它既是南北战争时期南方邦联的旗帜，也是一首 1880 年发行的著名福音歌曲。

# 译后记

.

自不量力，又鼓足勇气，我将《鲍勃·迪伦诗歌集》予以重译与修正，本意是想给中文读者提供一版或许更准确的中译。对首译者而言，这可能是冒犯，但也顾不得了。我想，译者的使命是对得起作者，使其作品能较少失真地面对其他语言地区的读者。至于其他"次生灾害"，都在其次。

想法归想法，能达成多少，不由译者说了算。聊以自慰的是，至少它与之前不同，可以提供另一种选择；认真的读者，疑惑时可以对照，从中或可得出可能的正解。

我的诗歌翻译观，基本来自北岛，即所谓"不增不减"。"不增不减"这四字，还可以说得更赤裸、更直白和更刻薄，就是译者绝不插手为作者做修饰，美化行为更加不可，唯以传递本义、本相貌为职责。但随着翻译数量的增多，我自己也在"蜕变"，对"不增不减"渐渐有了一些折中。比如，由于中英文的差异，语言习惯的不同，有时可以增减。但不可跨越的红线是，凡涉及与作品内涵、作品美学有关的部分，绝不更动，原作怎样就怎样。

我的诗歌翻译观还有第二个层面，即译者只翻译字面。这句话不太容易解释，可以打个比方：比如，我要向你介绍一首唐诗，正确的做法是我将唐诗原诗"端"给你，而不能给你讲唐诗的白话文释义。但英诗不是唐诗，原诗怎么"端"给你？其中的原则，相信你可以意会。

关于迪伦诗歌的翻译，还有第三个层面要交代。我通常都会直译，没办法直译时意译。关于诗歌直译和意译的关系，打起嘴仗来需要几本书，这里不赘述。但诗歌直译的好处，基于前面所讲的译诗观，即两个层面加起来，从逻辑上应该可以得出：直译是比较尊重作者以及作者母语的翻译方式。

涉及迪伦诗歌的具体翻译，还必须提及：这些诗歌原本是歌词，大多数时候更近于口语，所以我用大白话译，觉得这样最准。迪伦这个人，做什么都快。他的诗歌，往往以轻和直白，表达许多意思。那些大白话的诗句下，经常有潜台词。这是我的经验——他的作品需要慢读，需要反复读，只有如此你才能读到那些潜台词；如果把它们变成雅致的书面语，潜台词就会藏得很深，可能看不出来了。

诗歌翻译还有一个难题，就是如何解决押韵问题。我的译诗习惯是不刻意求押韵，在译成中文的过程中，自然地形成中文的诗韵。有时候，这种"自然地形成"受到原诗韵律的带动，相应地形成了中文的韵脚模式。有时候，韵脚和韵律是中文语言自己生成的。既符合原韵又符合原意的译诗，在我看来多数时候是不可能的，所以要解决这个不可解决的矛盾，只能是让句意优先，使押韵让位于意思，然后在中文语境下自然形成韵脚、韵律、节奏，从而形成令人赏心悦目的中文白话诗。这就是诗歌翻译的再创造，因为，谈及诗歌的诗意，占据第一位的首先是句意，诗意主要产生于句意，而非主要产生于押韵。过分讲究押韵，势必削足适履，扭曲和损害原诗，造出不自然的中文句子。所以这一部迪伦诗歌译本，在韵脚方面采取的策略完全是自由主义的。作为歌词，迪伦的韵脚原本非常讲究，有时极密，这只有请读者去对照原诗，以明白迪伦在歌唱方面的考虑。要了解这部分，还有一个至简的方法，就是打开音频，听歌。

事关翻译，最后还有个小说明，并非与翻译全然无关，那就是：本书的注释均采取了"非必要不注释"的原则。只有在不注释即影响阅读和理解的条件下，才做注释。因此，迪伦诗歌中可能与传统民歌、前人诗歌、文学和电影、《圣经》等有关的部分，能不注释则不注释。有时候，诗歌与所引对象的关系并不重要，读者完全可以通过阅读和倾听作品本身，获得对作品的理解。

鲍勃·迪伦是我深爱的诗人，对，是诗人，而不是诗人歌手。关于他的诗才、诗歌成就，尤其是他的作品够不够格，早不该在我们的讨论范围内。我很少看到一位诗人可以有那么多风格演变，他在不同时期创造出因应这一时期的、风格完全不同的诗歌，在思想上和情感上都发生了深刻的变化。像伟大的中国诗人杜甫一样，迪伦也是一位"诗史"型诗人。自 20 世纪 60 年代开始至今，长达 60 年时间，他一直在用他的作品反映时代，至今也还未停止。恰巧，这是人类历史上急剧动荡、极其丰富的时代，就这个时代本身而言，在整个人类历史上也是少有的。迪伦作品是关于这个时代最大的一面镜子，不只在歌曲史上，也在诗歌史上、文学史和艺术史上。由于迪伦所带动的潮流，以及他在时代潮流、世界文化中显赫的位置，迪伦的作品是对绝大多数人都有效的一面镜子。从中，我们不仅可以看到迪伦的形象，也可以看到我们自己的形象，不止一个，不止一面。

这套诗集中，在迪伦的每一辑作品前，我都写了一篇介绍。我本意是想力求客观，尽可能地呈现而非评判，但因为能力低微，有时做不到客观，只好"光着膀子"自己跳出来。然而我也发现，对迪伦这个人，我们其实所知不多，他很好地隐藏了自己，有时以在公共领域隐身的方式，有时以花枝招展的"迷魂阵"的方式。总之，关于他的生平，关于他的作品与时代的对应关系，大多数时候都还隐含在作品中，并未完全显露出来。

这套《鲍勃·迪伦诗歌集》的重译受益于所有的首译者，在此，谨向所有的译者致意，没有你们的先期翻译和研究，凭我一己之力，完成它是不可能的。这套书还收录了鲍勃·迪伦于 2020 年发行的新专辑，该专辑由顾悦先生首次翻译，在此向他致以敬意。我还要感谢郝佳先生，作为我最早的校译者，他给了我最大的帮助，甚至，是他教会了我如何尽可能准确地翻译。有些篇目，比如《没事儿，妈（我不过是在流血）》，若非他伸以援手，我完全得不到正确的理解。说到底，这首诗他才是第一译者，我顶多算第二译者。另外，在我完成这套诗集全部最初的译稿时，为了避免犯错误，我请教了杨盈盈，她对我的译稿以及已出版的部分迪伦诗歌译稿做了通读，指出了译文中的一些盲点，那是只有对摇滚乐史和迪伦个人史有深度了解的人才能够发现的，在此对她致以深深的谢意。

最后，我还要感谢中信出版集团，感谢本书编辑将如此重任交付于我，并给予我充分的信任。她们细心的编辑工作不仅减少了我的差错，也使文字增色不少。

李皖

2024 年 4 月 8 日